Iran's Nuclear Policy and the IAEA

An Evaluation of Program 93+2

Chen Zak

Military Research Papers no. 3

The Washington Institute for Near East Policy

Published in 2002 in the United States of America by The Washington Institute for Near East Policy, 1828 L Street NW, Suite 1050, Washington, DC 20036.

Library of Congress Cataloging-in-Publication Data

Zak, Chen, 1974–
Iran's nuclear policy and the IAEA: an evaluation of Program 93+2 / Chen Zak.
p. cm.—(Military research paper; no. 3)
Includes bibliographical references.
ISBN 0-944029-79-5
1. Nuclear arms control—Verification—Iran. 2. Nuclear weapons—Iran. 3. Nuclear nonproliferation. 4. International Atomic Energy Agency. I. Title: International Atomic Energy Agency and Iran's nuclear program. II. Title. III. Series.
UA12.5.Z34 2002
327.1'747'0955—dc21 2002006560
CIP

Cover design by Monica Neal Hertzman and Alicia Gansz. Additional cover art provided by Equator Graphics, Inc.

About the Author

Chen Zak served in the external affairs division of the Israeli Atomic Energy Commission (IAEC) from 1995 to 2000. Prior to joining the IAEC, she completed military service as an officer in the Israel Defense Forces.

Ms. Zak was a 2001 visiting fellow at The Washington Institute for Near East Policy and is currently a researcher at the Center for Strategic and International Studies. She earned a bachelor's degree in sociology, anthropology, and political science from Tel Aviv University, where she also completed a master's degree in security studies. Most recently, Ms. Zak earned a master's degree in law and diplomacy from the Fletcher School of Law and Diplomacy, Tufts University. Currently, she is a doctoral candidate at the Fletcher School, concentrating on international law and security studies.

• • •

The views expressed in this paper are those of the author and should not be construed as representing those of the Israeli Atomic Energy Commission; the Center for Strategic and International Studies; or The Washington Institute for Near East Policy, its Board of Trustees, or its Board of Advisors.

Table of Contents

Acknowledgments

So many have lent their assistance during the writing of this paper. It is impossible to mention them all, but in particular I would like to thank The Washington Institute for Near East Policy and its director for policy and strategic planning, Robert Satloff, for making my fellowship at the Institute possible.

Special thanks go to Patrick Clawson, Michael Eisenstadt, and other readers from the Israeli Atomic Energy Commission for their comments and wise counsel in reviewing and improving this paper; Ephraim Asculai and Shai Feldman for reading the paper in its initial stages and providing invaluable suggestions; and Gideon Frank, Itzhak Lederman, Ze'ev Schiff, and Ariel Levite for their support and encouragement over the course of my career.

The proofreaders of the various drafts, Assaf Moghadam and Mariya Kravkova, helped to polish my writing; but I want to thank them more for being good friends. I am also grateful to Alicia Gansz and George Lopez for their editing skills and patient efforts in producing this study.

Some additional work related to the theoretical sections of this paper was completed at the Fletcher School of Law and Diplomacy. I am grateful to Richard Shultz for his support and advice.

Last, but by no means least, I want to thank my two brothers, Shaul and Or, and my sister, Shaked, for their steadfast encouragement throughout my education and every day of my life.

Finally, this book is dedicated to my mother, the most devoted and loving person I have ever known. Her encouragement gave me the strength to follow my dreams by approaching every challenge as an adventure, and her guidance was indispensable in completing this project.

Chen Zak
Washington, D.C.
June 2002

Preface

Regrettably, the passing of the Cold War did not end the threat of nuclear war. Indeed, in an era of U.S.-Russian cooperation against common threats of terrorism and proliferation, the world may be more reliant on systems of global arms control than ever before.

But the record of these international regimes in protecting against "rogue" nuclear weapons programs does not inspire confidence. In the early 1990s, the global arms control community was severely shaken by the belated discovery that two signatories to the Treaty on the Non-Proliferation of Nuclear Weapons (NPT)—Iraq and North Korea—possessed advanced clandestine nuclear weapons programs. Although the International Atomic Energy Agency (IAEA) certified as late as April 1990 that Iraq was in full compliance with its NPT obligations, post–Gulf War intelligence information and special inspections revealed that Iraq's prewar clandestine nuclear program employed 20,000 and cost $10–15 billion. In response to these challenges and to enhance its inspections capability, the IAEA adopted a strengthened safeguards regime known as "Program 93+2."

Currently, the Islamic Republic of Iran provides a good test case for evaluating the potential role of Program 93+2 in addressing the problem of nuclear proliferation. Although Western intelligence agencies maintain that Iran does, in fact, possess a nuclear weapons program—which Iranian officials deny—verification measures open to the IAEA remain limited since the country has so far refused to fully adopt the new safeguards regime.

The Washington Institute is pleased to present Chen Zak's detailed examination of Program 93+2 and of whether this new regime—when fully adopted by Iran—would allow detection of Iranian nuclear weapons development. Her study addresses a larger issue for U.S. policy, namely, whether the international community has developed a system adequate to detect rogue nuclear weapons programs. Ms. Zak also explores an arms control alternative that could prove more effective than the IAEA: an agreement among Middle Eastern states—once peace treaties are achieved among the countries of the region—designating the Middle East as a nuclear weapons–free zone, with each state having the right to inspect the others.

Now at Tufts University, Chen Zak began her examination of the IAEA's Program 93+2 while working at the Israeli Atomic Energy Commission, and resumed her analysis of the issue as a 2001 visiting fellow at The Washington Institute. Her study should be read by all those concerned about finding ways to control the proliferation of nuclear weapons in the Middle East.

Michael Stein
Chairman

Fred S. Lafer
President

Executive Summary

Thwarting Iran's ambitions to acquire nuclear weapons has been a key focus of nuclear nonproliferation efforts since the early 1990s. These efforts were given new urgency by President George W. Bush's January 29, 2002, State of the Union address, which identified Iranian nuclear weapons development as a threat that the United States would not tolerate.

In addition to Iran, the nuclear arms–control community has faced two other serious challenges since the early 1990s: Iraq and North Korea. In 1991, following the Gulf War, the International Atomic Energy Agency (IAEA) discovered that Iraq had developed an advanced nuclear weapons program, although the country was (and still is) a party to the Treaty on the Non-Proliferation of Nuclear Weapons (NPT) and was outwardly in full compliance with its safeguards obligations. In 1993, North Korea threatened to withdraw from the NPT while refusing to accept an IAEA special inspection aimed at verifying the discrepancies in its declaration. The need for a more effective IAEA safeguards regime emerged with the revelation that these two NPT parties, each bound by a comprehensive safeguards agreement, had succeeded in developing a clandestine nuclear weapons program.

This study presents and evaluates the IAEA's strengthened safeguards system known as "Program 93+2," appraising the system's capabilities and limitations as well as its potential for contributing to nuclear nonproliferation efforts in the Middle East generally, and in Iran in particular.

Program 93+2 was designed to strengthen the IAEA's verification capacity with regard to nonnuclear weapons states on two fronts: preventing the diversion of declared materials and detecting undeclared activities in those states. The program was adopted and implemented by the agency in three phases.

The first phase, concluded in 1992, includes a voluntary universal reporting system for transfers of nuclear equipment and specified nonnuclear materials; affirmation of the IAEA's right to conduct special inspections with the full backing of the United Nations Security Council (UNSC); and the right of the agency to use all available information sources, including intelligence. The second phase was adopted by the IAEA in 1995 and included measures that, although falling under the existing IAEA mandate, had not been implemented by the agency.

In May 1997, the IAEA approved the Additional Protocol, the final stage of Program 93+2, adopted primarily to strengthen the agency's ability to detect undeclared activities in nonnuclear weapons states. All states party to the NPT are asked to adopt this instrument as a complement to their full-scope safeguards agreement. The Additional Protocol imposes additional obligations on these states and enlarges the IAEA's mandate in the following ways:

1. *States are required to submit an expanded declaration to the agency*. Under the Additional Protocol, all buildings on a particular site must be declared and identified, regardless of use. States are also required to include in their declarations all nuclear-related activities—past, present, and future, peaceful or not, with or without the presence of nuclear materials.

2. *IAEA inspectors are granted expanded access rights, including access to nuclear-related locations at which nuclear materials are not necessarily present (e.g., university laboratories).* The IAEA also has the authority to conduct location-specific and wide-area environmental sampling to verify the absence of activities that fall outside the scope of a state's declaration.

Program 93+2 represents an important step in strengthening the IAEA's verification capabilities. The program can and should bring about a more reliable verification regime aimed at preventing a recurrence of the Iraq and North Korea experiences. It is therefore important to encourage all IAEA member states, especially those of concern such as Iran, to fully adopt the program's Additional Protocol.

Limitations of the New Safeguards System

At the same time, it is important to note some limitations of the new safeguards system that might affect future nonproliferation efforts. First, Program 93+2 and its Additional Protocol address only some of the paths available to a state pursuing the clandestine development of nuclear weapons. Although the existence of unaddressed paths is a serious concern, the related problems (and their solutions) are concentrated at the political and legal—not the technical or safeguards—levels, and thus fall outside the IAEA mandate and the scope of this paper.

Second, the effectiveness of future IAEA verification efforts with regard to the paths covered by the Additional Protocol will largely depend on the agency's decisiveness, as well as the political support it receives from both IAEA member states and the UNSC. Under the old safeguards system, the IAEA conducted verification missions according to nondiscrimination criteria, spending 80 percent of its inspections efforts in states whose highly developed nuclear energy programs did not raise proliferation concerns (e.g., Canada, Japan, and members of the European Community).

Under the Additional Protocol, the IAEA can become proactive, conducting verification efforts that focus less on nondiscrimination criteria and more on a country's nonproliferation credentials. If, instead, the IAEA continues to adhere to its traditional, event-driven safeguards policy, states may employ various deception and denial techniques to conceal their attempts to develop nuclear weapons.

Third, it is important to note that even under the Additional Protocol, the IAEA's ability to detect undeclared activities, especially those taking place at undeclared sites, remains limited. Indeed, the new technical tools available to the IAEA under the protocol (e.g., wide-area environmental sampling and satellite imagery) will have limited effectiveness if the agency does not have prior information as to the specific locations of the undeclared activities.

Iran's Policy toward the Additional Protocol as a Test Case

The Iranian challenge provides a fascinating case for proliferation analysts. Iran is the only state in the Middle East that is party to all nonproliferation agreements; yet, many suspect that the country has never abandoned its attempts to acquire weapons of mass destruction, including the long-range missiles used to deliver them. The five leading intelligence organizations (those of the United States, the United Kingdom, France, Germany, and Israel) have warned that Iran is developing a clandestine nuclear weapons program. Yet, the IAEA has found that country to be in full compliance with its safeguards agreement; the agency has neither detected violations of Iran's treaty obligations, nor exposed any clandestine Iranian nuclear weapons program.

Because Iran rejects any allegations that it is developing a nuclear weapons program, its policy toward the Additional Protocol can be viewed as a test case with regard to the country's NPT and other nonproliferation commitments. If Tehran does not intend to develop a clandestine program, it will delay signing by making its signature conditional upon maximizing political gains, technical cooperation, and economic support.

If Iran chooses to embark on a nuclear weapons program, it will avoid signing the Additional Protocol as long as it can resist the consequent political and technological pressure, which is currently limited. Moreover, it will most likely sign (but not ratify) the Additional Protocol only after it overcomes all technical obstacles to the production of a nuclear weapon, obtains all the necessary resources, and, most likely, begins to produce fissile material. Therefore, until Iran fully accedes to and complies with the Additional Protocol, the international community should both press Iran to fully adopt the protocol and prevent the country from receiving any political, technical, or economic benefits in the meantime.

Should Iran decide to sign the Additional Protocol, it will likely avoid ratification. By signing without ratifying, Iran could secure the benefits of a signatory (and be considered a party in good faith) without being obliged to the protocol legally or technically. In this case, the IAEA would not have the right to employ the verification measures provided by the protocol, thus restricting the agency's ability to ensure Iranian compliance. In fact, until Iran ratifies the Additional Protocol, the country's de facto safeguards obligations will remain limited to INFCIRC/153 (the IAEA's full-scope safeguards agreement). Since the Iranian government has not yet incorporated Part 1 measures from Program 93+2, Iran's safeguards status is currently identical to that of Iraq prior to the Gulf War.

Even in the unlikely event that Iran decides to ratify the protocol, it is highly improbable that the IAEA would be able to detect illicit activities in undeclared sites that do not intersect with the country's safeguarded civil nuclear program if no specific information on the violation (a "smoking gun") is provided by IAEA member states. Therefore, if Iran enters directly or indirectly into negotiations with the IAEA for adopting the protocol, any resulting agreement should include a timetable for both signature and ratification. This kind of precaution would reduce, but not fully eliminate, the possibility of Iran misusing the verification regime.

A Regional Approach as an Alternative?

The Iran case provides an opportunity not only to examine the potential role of the Additional Protocol in addressing the problem of nuclear proliferation, but also to compare the effectiveness of the protocol with other alternate systems—specifically, a regional nonproliferation regime.

The regional approach may be a better option for the Middle East than an international verification regime because it offers the flexibility of adopting measures more relevant to the region, such as mutual inspection and lower thresholds for the triggering of safeguards. Given the special circumstances of the Middle East—where a relatively small amount of nuclear material exists and suspicions about noncompliance are high—these kinds of measures would not only increase a regional regime's ability to prevent the diversion of material sufficient to develop a nuclear device, but also strengthen the confidence of member states in the regime's ability to detect violators.

Because today a regional approach in the Middle East seems more hypothetical than ever, the Additional Protocol remains the best available mechanism in the region for restricting a state's ability to develop nuclear weapons. Although no system is foolproof, a stronger IAEA verification regime can build barriers and raise the price that Iran or any other state must pay—in money, time, and manpower—in order to successfully develop a clandestine nuclear program.

Acronyms

ABACC—Brazilian-Argentine Agency for Accounting and Control of Nuclear Materials
ACRS—Arms Control and Regional Security working group
AEOI—Atomic Energy Organization of Iran
CWC—Chemical Weapons Convention
DIV—Design information verification
EURATOM—European Atomic Energy Community
GSCR—Graphite Subcritical Reactor
HWZPR—Heavy-Water Zero-Power Reactor 1
IAEA—International Atomic Energy Agency
INFCIRC—IAEA information circular
INFCIRC/66—IAEA location-specific safeguards system (1965)
INFCIRC/153—IAEA model full-scope safeguards agreement
INFCIRC/214—Iran's NPT safeguards agreement with the IAEA
INFCIRC/540—IAEA Additional Protocol of Program 93+2
LOF—Location outside facility
LWSCR—Light-Water Subcritical Reactor
MNSR—Miniature Neutron Source Reactor 1
NNWS—Nonnuclear weapons state
NPT—Treaty on the Non-Proliferation of Nuclear Weapons
NSG—Nuclear Supplier Group
NWFZ—Nuclear weapons–free zone
NWS—Nuclear weapons state (as defined by the NPT)
OPANAL—Agency for the Prohibition of Nuclear Weapons in Latin America and the Caribbean
OPCW—Organization for the Prohibition of Chemical Weapons
R&D—Research and development
SAGSI—Standing Advisory Group on Safeguards Implementation
SSAC—State system of accounting and control
TRR—Research Reactor 1 (Tehran)
UNSCOM—United Nations Special Commission
UNSC—United Nations Security Council
WMD—Weapons of mass destruction
WMDFZ—Weapons of mass destruction–free zone

Introduction

Thwarting Iran's ambitions to acquire nuclear weapons has been a key focus of nuclear nonproliferation efforts since the early 1990s. These efforts were given new urgency by President George W. Bush's January 29, 2002, State of the Union address, which identified Iranian nuclear weapons development as a threat that the United States would not tolerate.

In addition to Iran, the nuclear arms–control community has faced two other serious challenges since the early 1990s: Iraq and North Korea. In 1991, following the Gulf War, the International Atomic Energy Agency (IAEA) discovered that Iraq had developed an advanced nuclear weapons program, although it had been a party to the Treaty on the Non-Proliferation of Nuclear Weapons (NPT) and was outwardly in full compliance with its safeguards agreement obligations. In 1993, North Korea threatened to withdraw from the NPT while refusing to accept an IAEA special inspection to verify the discrepancies in its declaration. The need for a more effective IAEA safeguards regime emerged with the revelation that these two NPT parties, each bound by a comprehensive safeguards agreement, had succeeded in developing a clandestine nuclear weapons program.

This study will present and evaluate the IAEA's strengthened safeguards system, known as "Program 93+2," appraising its capabilities and limitations as well as its potential for contributing to nuclear nonproliferation efforts in the Middle East generally, and in Iran in particular.

The study is divided into four sections. Chapter 1 describes the challenges that nuclear nonproliferation efforts—particularly the IAEA safeguards system—have faced since the early 1990s. Chapter 2 evaluates Program 93+2 and the measures adopted under this new safeguards system. Chapter 3 assesses Iranian policy toward Program 93+2 under two possible scenarios: (1) Iran decides not to develop nuclear weapons and fully complies with its arms control obligations, or (2) Iran takes steps toward the development of a clandestine nuclear program. Chapter 4 compares the NPT safeguards regime, which is implemented by an international organization (the IAEA), with an alternative verification regime based on a regional agreement. The relative advantages and disadvantages of applying the two kinds of regimes in a region like the Middle East, where suspicions about weapons of mass destruction (WMD) development are high, warrant examination.

This study will not attempt to assess Iranian nuclear capabilities, but will instead evaluate the possible stances that Iran might adopt with regard to its nuclear program.

Chapter 1

Challenges to Nonproliferation Efforts

The NPT, which was signed in 1968, divides states party to the treaty into two groups: countries that "have manufactured and exploded a nuclear weapon or other nuclear explosive device prior to 1 January, 1967," known as nuclear weapons states (NWSs)[1]; and all other states, known as nonnuclear weapons states (NNWSs). According to the NPT, NNWSs agree not to "manufacture or otherwise acquire nuclear weapons or other nuclear explosive devices."[2] In order to verify this commitment, each NNWS party to the treaty undertakes to place all source materials and special fissile material used in peaceful nuclear activities under IAEA safeguards.

When the NPT entered into force in 1970, the IAEA developed a model safeguards agreement (IAEA document INFCIRC/153[3]) to be used as a basis for all safeguards agreements with NNWS signatories to the NPT. It is a comprehensive (full-scope) agreement, designed to cover the entire fuel cycle of NNWSs. The purpose of the safeguards is to ensure that material declared by NNWSs as being used for peaceful purposes is not diverted to the development of nuclear weapons.[4]

The 1970 IAEA verification regime was limited in its scope, intended to ensure only the correctness of the signatories' declarations regarding the peaceful use of nuclear material and activities, not the completeness of those declarations. Specifically, the IAEA system was designed to verify whether signatories' declarations corresponded with their declared installations and activities; it was not designed to detect either undeclared installations or activities, or the existence of an independent, clandestine nuclear program that did not intersect with the declared activities.

These limitations on the IAEA's mandate were rooted in a common postulate that had long guided the arms control community—namely, that if a state should choose to pursue a nuclear weapons program, either it would not sign the NPT in the first place or its activities would eventually be detected. The rationale behind this assumption was that the amount of nuclear material diverted for a weapon would be sizable, and that the clandestine program would be too large and too difficult to keep secret.[5] Indeed, at the time the IAEA was established, nuclear weapons development was thought to

> require at the minimum several hundred scientists and a great deal of equipment. Such large-scale projects, running several years, are difficult to conceal from the CIA [Central Intelligence Agency] and its equivalents elsewhere, with their thoroughgoing techniques and elaborate mechanical and electronic devices. Thus, it may be possible to detect nuclear development without official inspection and without espionage in some cases. In short, a non-nuclear state seeking to obtain nuclear weapons furtively has a rather poor chance of proceeding undetected.[6]

But these assumptions proved false in the early 1990s when the IAEA safeguards system faced three serious challenges:

1. *The 1991 revelation that Iraq, although party to the NPT and outwardly in full compliance with its safeguards agreement*

obligations, had developed an extensive nuclear weapons program. The IAEA's failure to expose the immense $10–15 billion Iraqi program—which involved thirty or more sites, a staff of 20,000, and a clandestine enrichment program—revealed the limitations of the safeguards regime as well as its loopholes. Indeed, following the last routine IAEA inspection in Iraq (in April 1990, a few months before the Iraqi invasion of Kuwait), IAEA safeguards division director Jon Jennekens called the cooperation of Iraqi nuclear officials with the IAEA "exemplary." "Iraq's nuclear experts," Jennekens said, "have made every effort to demonstrate that Iraq is a solid citizen" in the NPT regime.[7]

In the wake of the 1991 Gulf War ceasefire, the United Nations Security Council (UNSC), acting under Chapter VII of the UN Charter, adopted Resolutions 687 and 707, establishing two verification bodies: the IAEA Action Team, responsible for monitoring the clandestine development of nuclear weapons; and the United Nations Special Commission (UNSCOM), responsible for monitoring chemical and biological weapons, as well as missiles. The IAEA was entrusted with extensive rights and privileges to destroy, remove, or render harmless the entire Iraqi nuclear program. The access rights granted to the IAEA Action Team (which differ widely from the routine inspections conducted by the IAEA in NNWSs) were highly intrusive in comparison to any safeguards agreements to which a sovereign state would ever voluntarily agree.[8]

2. *The 1993 threat by North Korea to withdraw from the NPT, along with Pyongyang's refusal to accept an IAEA special inspection to verify the discrepancies in its initial declaration.* A different approach was taken in the North Korean crisis: when North Korea refused to allow the IAEA to conduct

a special inspection, the agency declared the country to be in noncompliance with its safeguards obligations. In accordance with the IAEA Statute, the agency then transferred the report of noncompliance to the UNSC. Following China's threat to block a UNSC decision supporting the IAEA special inspection request, however, North Korea and the United States signed an agreed framework in October 1994. The agreement outlined a formula designed to introduce—in its last phase—the complete dismantling of North Korea's nuclear weapons program; in exchange, the United States and its allies would construct two modern light-water reactors and supply North Korea with heavy-fuel oil for the duration of the period in which the reactors were to be constructed. In addition, the United States offered diplomatic recognition to North Korea and an end to U.S. economic sanctions.

3. *Current accusations that Iran is using its NPT membership as a cover to develop a clandestine nuclear program.* The IAEA's Safeguards Implementation Report has found Iran to be in full compliance with its safeguards agreement obligations.[9] The agency has not detected any Iranian violations, nor has it exposed an Iranian nuclear weapons program. Yet, the five leading intelligence organizations (those of the United States, the United Kingdom, France, Germany, and Israel) have warned that Iran is indeed developing nuclear weapons in parallel with its safeguarded civil nuclear program.[10]

Iran rejects these allegations and vigorously stresses that, in the absence of proof for such claims, any restrictions on the transfer of nuclear-related technology to Iran are illegal under the NPT.[11] Iranian officials specifically refer to Article IV of the NPT, which guarantees the right of all signatories "to develop research, production and use of nuclear energy for peaceful purposes without discrimination." Moreover, according to the article, all parties to the treaty have a right "to participate in the fullest possible exchange of equipment, materials and scientific and technological information for the peaceful uses of nuclear energy . . . especially in the territories of non-nuclear-weapon States Party to the Treaty, with due consideration for the needs of the developing areas of the world."[12]

Iran claims to be in full compliance with its NPT obligations. Yet, important questions remain concerning the extent of the country's nuclear program and its policy toward the new IAEA safeguards, particularly the Additional Protocol of Program 93+2 (discussed in chapter 2). The Iranian case provides an important opportunity to examine the role of the Additional Protocol in addressing regional proliferation concerns, as well as possible alternate means of addressing those concerns. Because Iran rejects allegations that it is developing a nuclear weapons program, its policy toward the Additional Protocol can also be viewed as a test case with regard to Iran's NPT and other nonproliferation commitments.

Notes

1. "Treaty on the Non-Proliferation of Nuclear Weapons," no. 10485 in *United Nations Treaty Series*, vol. 729 (New York: United Nations, 1968), pp. 169–75, Article IX, para. 3. The text of the treaty is also available online (www.unog.ch/disarm/distreat/npt.pdf).

2. Ibid., Article II.

3. *The Structure and Content of Agreements between the Agency and States Required in Connection with the Treaty on the Non-Proliferation of Nuclear Weapons* (IAEA document INFCIRC/153 [Corrected]). Available online (www.iaea.org/worldatom/Documents/Infcircs/Others/inf153.shtml).

4. "Treaty on the Non-Proliferation of Nuclear Weapons," Article III.

5. David Kay, "Iraq and Beyond: Future Nonproliferation Inspection Challenges" (Nonproliferation Policy Education Center, March 1996). Available online (www.npec-web.org/essay/kay.htm). David Kay served as team leader for several IAEA inspections in Iraq.

6. Steven Rosen, "Proliferation Treaty Controls and the IAEA," *Journal of Conflict Resolution* 11, no. 2 (April 1967), p. 174.

7. Mark Hibbs and Ann Maclachlan, "No Bomb-Quantity of HEU in Iraq, IAEA Safeguards Report Indicates," *Nuclear Fuel* 15, no. 17 (August 20, 1990), p. 8.

8. It is troubling to note that, while the Operation Desert Storm target list on January 6, 1991, included only two nuclear-related Iraqi facilities (only one of which had been inspected prior to the Gulf War), UNSCOM and the IAEA Action Team together uncovered more than thirty Iraqi nuclear-related sites. See Federation of American Scientists, "Iraqi Special Weapons Facilities," in *Iraq Special Weapons Guide*, n.d. Available online (www.fas.org/nuke/guide/iraq/facility).

9. In June 2001, the IAEA board of governors reviewed the implementation of IAEA safeguards in 2000. According to the IAEA, "[I]n the 140 States . . . which have safeguards agreements in force, nuclear material and other items placed under safeguards remained in peaceful nuclear activities or were otherwise adequately accounted for. . . . [T]he Agency found no indication of diversion of nuclear material placed under safeguards or of misuse of facilities, equipment or non-nuclear material placed under safeguards." From "IAEA Board Reviews Record of Safeguards Implementation," IAEA press release, PR 2001/14 (June 18, 2001). Available online (www.iaea.org/worldatom/Press/P_release/2001/prn0114.shtml).

10. Western intelligence reports since the early 1990s have asserted that Iran is attempting not only to develop the capability to produce plutonium and highly enriched uranium, but also to procure equipment and technology for its nuclear program. Various intelligence agencies claim that Iran has also tried to obtain fissile material secretly from former Soviet inventories, from China, and from North Korea. See, for example, *Unclassified Report to Congress on the Acquisition of Technology Relating to Weapons*

of Mass Destruction and Advanced Conventional Munitions, 1 July through 31 December 2000, available online (www.cia.gov/cia/publications/bian/bian_sep_2001.htm); *Statement by Deputy Director, DCI Nonproliferation Center, A. Norman Schindler on Iran's Weapons of Mass Destruction Programs to the International Security, Proliferation and Federal Services Subcommittee of the Senate Governmental Affairs Committee,* September 21, 2000, available online (www.cia.gov/cia/public_affairs/speeches/archives/2000/schindler_WMD_092200.htm); Mark Hibbs, "Iran Said To Be Stepping Up Effort To Support Laser Enrichment Program," *Nuclear Fuel* 23, no. 20 (October 5, 1998), p. 1; Mark Hibbs, "Iran Sought Sensitive Nuclear Supplies from Argentina and China," *Nucleonics Week* 33, no. 39 (September 24, 1993), p. 2; and Mark Hibbs, "Witness to Sting Operation Claims Iran Sought Warheads," *Nucleonics Week* 38, no. 35 (August 28, 1997), p. 16.

11. See Mohamed Sadegh Ayatollahi, "Iran Replies to the Risk Report; Denies It Wants the Bomb," *Risk Report* 2, no. 1 (January–February 1996), pp. 2–3, available online (www.wisconsinproject.org/countries/iran/denies.html); and "Iran Denies Seeking Nuclear Weapons," Reuters, September 10, 2001.

12. "Treaty on the Non-Proliferation of Nuclear Weapons," Article IV.

Chapter 2

The New Safeguards Regime: Program 93+2

The revelation of the Iraqi and North Korean nuclear programs left no doubt that IAEA operations under the 1970 IAEA verification regime (INFCIRC/153) were insufficient and limited to verifying only the nondiversion of substantial amounts of declared materials. In fact, it was intelligence information provided to the IAEA by the United States that exposed both programs. Even the Iraqi "crash program"—aimed at diverting safeguarded nuclear fuel and recovering from it highly enriched uranium for use in a nuclear weapon—was brought to light neither by the special, intrusive verification mandate that the IAEA and UNSCOM received under UNSC Resolution 687, nor by the IAEA's routine inspection before the Gulf War. Rather, it was uncovered only after the defection of Hussein Kamel, the head of Iraq's special-weapons program, in August 1995.

Inevitable questions arose in the wake of these discoveries: are Iraq and North Korea unique, or are other IAEA member states also developing clandestine nuclear programs? This possibility required a reevaluation of the IAEA's mandate and of the "culture of trust" that the agency had been maintaining with regard to compliance.

In response, the IAEA initiated a program to expand its verification mandate and capabilities. These new measures were affirmed gradually. The first phase, adopted by the IAEA board of governors in 1992, called for a universal reporting system under which all parties were invited to voluntarily notify the IAEA about transfers of nuclear equipment and specified nonnuclear materials. The board hoped that the provision of such data on exports, imports, and the production of nuclear materials would help to create a "closed system" containing the global balancing of source materials. The board also affirmed the right of the IAEA to conduct special inspections with the full backing of the UNSC, should the agency's request for a special inspection be denied.

In addition, the board approved the use of all available information sources during IAEA inspections, including intelligence provided by member states (called "national technical means"), which had not been utilized before the Iraqi and North Korean experiences. In the shadow of these two cases, two technologies have proven especially valuable: satellite imagery and environmental monitoring (also called "high-performance trace analysis").

Satellite pictures provided to the IAEA by the United States have at times constituted primary evidence for the agency's suspicions and subsequent inspections; for instance, U.S. satellite imagery ultimately led to both the discovery of two undeclared storage facilities in North Korea and a determination of the true size of Iraq's al-Tuwaitha nuclear site (see p. 50). Although commercial satellite imagery, unlike national technical means, is not in and of itself capable of detecting undeclared nuclear activities, it has significant potential for uncovering discrepancies that the IAEA may then attempt to resolve by special inspections and complementary or managed access.[1]

With regard to environmental monitoring, the IAEA has stated the following:

> Any production or manufacturing process loses some small fraction of [its] materials to the immediate envi-

> ronment. . . . [N]uclear materials have specific physical properties (e.g., radioactivity) that make it possible to detect and characterize extremely small quantities. This capability—together with the possibility that specific [isotopic] signatures can be unambiguously correlated with specific nuclear processes—is why environmental monitoring is seen as having promise with respect to the detection of undeclared activities.[2]

In parallel to its adoption of the above-mentioned measures, the IAEA also mandated the Standing Advisory Group on Safeguards Implementation (SAGSI) to explore ways of enhancing the agency's ability to detect undeclared activities at an early stage. The result was the initiation of Program 93+2, so named because it was initiated in 1993 ("93") and was expected to conclude two years later ("+2") in 1995, prior to the NPT Review and Extension Conference. The declared aim of this program was "to strengthen the safeguards system and in particular to develop its ability to detect and to have access to undeclared activities."[3] In contrast to the 1970 INFCIRC/153 agreement, the new safeguards system would seek to verify the absence of any undeclared activities and materials anywhere in a given state, not just in declared sites.

Program 93+2 was articulated by SAGSI in two separate documents. Part I included measures that fell under the IAEA mandate and thus could be implemented immediately.[4] Part II included measures that fell outside the IAEA mandate and thus required each state to approve them individually by adopting an "Additional Protocol" (also called "Model Protocol," or INFCIRC/540[5]) as an added instrument to the INFCIRC/153 safeguards agreement.

In other words, the Additional Protocol would act as a complementary legal document for states that already had a full-scope safeguards agreement with the IAEA.

According to Mohamed ElBaradei (current IAEA director general and, at the time of the protocol's design, assistant director general of the agency's external relations division), the Additional Protocol was not intended for use as a stand-alone document, first, because "no state could adhere to the protocol unless it had previously concluded a safeguards agreement with the agency," and second, because "the protocol depended in many ways on the underlying safeguards agreement."[6]

The Additional Protocol is a bilateral agreement between individual states and the IAEA, not a multilateral treaty. Thus, every NNWS must adopt the protocol unilaterally. In addition, there is neither a threshold—a minimal number of states required for the entry into force of the protocol—nor a timeframe within which INFCIRC/153 states must adopt the protocol.

Unilateral adoption has positive as well as negative implications. On the one hand, if a minimal number of states—or specific states[7]—were required for the protocol to enter into force, the significance of individual states would expand, and the political pressure on each to join would be extensive. Each state would be able to block the entry into force of the entire treaty (a tremendous power[8]) and would probably try to use this power as leverage to maximize political gains.

But the legal situation under the Additional Protocol is different. Because there is neither a minimal number of states nor a specific list of states needed to ratify the protocol, each state must, as noted, adopt the protocol independently of other states. In other words, each state is responsible only for the entry into force of its own agreement. Consequently, the political pressure that states can impose upon one another to adopt the protocol is limited.

As mentioned, the Additional Protocol was designed as a supplementary measure for INFCIRC/153 states. Nevertheless, other states—specifically, the five NPT nuclear weapons states (the United States, Russia, the United Kingdom, France, and China), and the four states not party to the NPT but having facility-specific safeguards agreements[9] (Cuba, India, Israel, and Pakistan)—are encouraged to adopt measures from the protocol that they identify as capable of contributing to the nonproliferation effort.[10] As of May 2002, all five NWSs had signed the Additional Protocol, but only China had ratified it. Among the four non-NPT states, only Cuba had signed (though it had not yet ratified) the protocol (see appendix 3).

The approved Program 93+2, in both its parts, encompasses complementary activities vital to resolving questions about the correctness and completeness of the information provided in a state's declaration, as well as resolving inconsistencies relating to that information. In general, the additional measures cover three fields:

1. *Expansion of the information that states must provide to the agency.* The declarations that states are required to submit under Program 93+2 cover a much broader range than required under INFCIRC/153, going beyond nuclear material and facilities containing nuclear material. INFCIRC/153 states are required to submit a declaration covering only nuclear materials, associated processes (if contained nuclear materials need to be under safeguards), and nuclear facilities containing or expected to contain declared nuclear material; but under Program 93+2, all buildings on a particular site must be declared and identified, regardless of their use. The expanded information, in addition to certain verification activities, should "make a state's nuclear fuel cycle and associated activities more 'transparent.'"[11]

The expanded declaration represents a significant additional commitment in other ways as well. If, under INFCIRC/153, NNWSs are permitted to carry out unsafeguarded military nuclear programs (as long as they are not related to nuclear weapons or explosives) and are allowed to withdraw safeguarded material for nonproscribed military activities (as long as that material will not be used for the production of nuclear weapons or explosives), under Program 93+2 those states are required to file a complete declaration, including all nuclear-related activities—past, present, and future, peaceful or not, with or without the presence of nuclear materials.

2. *Expansion of access rights for the IAEA and its inspectors.* Access rights under INFCIRC/153 are limited to the "strategic points" in declared facilities. The IAEA selects these points by examining the design information of declared sites (or, in certain cases, the facilities themselves) and then designating locations at which the agency can obtain and verify the information necessary for implementing its safeguards measures. A strategic point may include any location where key measurements are taken and where containment and surveillance measures are executed.[12]

The Additional Protocol, rather, grants complementary access rights to the IAEA and its inspectors. With these expanded rights, inspectors have access to any location on a nuclear site, to mines, and to "nuclear-related locations" (as defined by the agency, "related to nuclear proliferation issues"),[13] even where no nuclear materials are present. The latter include, for example, universities at which nuclear research and development or manufacturing activities are carried out.

In order to verify the absence of undeclared nuclear material and activities under the expanded access rights of the Additional Protocol, the IAEA also has the authority to conduct environmental sampling. Toward this end, the IAEA may deploy location-specific environmental sampling (otherwise permitted only at strategic points) in a state, once technical feasibility is demonstrated and approved by the IAEA board of governors.

Another method of environmental sampling has also been approved: wide-area environmental sampling, which is aimed at establishing whether nuclear activities are present at sites to which the IAEA did not previously have access rights. Although the Additional Protocol recognizes the right of the IAEA to deploy such monitoring in order to search for nuclear indications over extensive areas (in contrast to location-specific monitoring), wide-area environmental sampling would be implemented only when the efficacy of the technology is established and the board of governors approves the circumstances, details, and analytical method of the sampling. In any case, future wide-area environmental sampling would be implemented as part of the Additional Protocol only after consultations with the state concerned.

3. *Streamlining of administrative procedures crucial to the effective implementation of safeguards.*[14] This includes, for example, procedural simplification for the designation of inspectors, and approval of multi-entry visas valid for at least one year. Multi-entry visas permit inspectors to enter a country without delay, thereby reducing the ability of the state to remove traces of illegitimate activity. Other measures adopted include the use of unattended, remote-monitoring equipment and new methods of communication between onsite inspectors and IAEA headquarters.

Notes

1. Hans Hermann Remagen and Bernd Richter, "Implications for Research and Development in Safeguards Technology," in *Tightening the Reins*, ed. Erwin Hackel and Gotthard Stein (Berlin: Springer, 2000), p. 123.

2. Bruno Pellaud and Richard Hooper, "IAEA Safeguards in the 1990s: Building from Experience," *IAEA Bulletin* 37, no. 1 (March 1997). Also available online (www.iaea.org/worldatom/Periodicals/Bulletin/Bull371/pellaud.html).

3. *The Annual Report for 1997* (Vienna: IAEA, 1998), p. 49. Also available online (www.iaea.org/cgi-bin/byteserver.pl/worldatom/inforesource/annual/anrep97/safeguards.pdf).

4. Adopted in *Strengthening the Effectiveness and Improving the Efficiency of the Safeguards System—Proposals for a Strengthened and More Efficient Safeguards System: A Report by the Director General* (IAEA document GOV/2807), May 12, 1995.

5. *Model Protocol Additional to the Agreement(s) between State(s) and the International Atomic Energy Agency for the Application of Safeguards* (IAEA document INFCIRC/540), September 1997. Available online (www.iaea.org/worldatom/Documents/Infcircs/1997/infcirc540.pdf).

6. Mohamed ElBaradei, "Interpretation by the Secretariat of the Relationship between the Protocol and the Safeguards Agreement," Attachment 2 (IAEA document GOV/2914), April 7, 1997. Available online (www.iaea.org/worldatom/About/GC/GC41/documents/2914attach2.html).

7. Modern multilateral arms control treaties tend to include a specific number or specific group of states that need to ratify the treaty before it could enter into force. For example, the Chemical Weapons Convention (CWC) had to be ratified by sixty-five states before it fully entered into force, while the Comprehensive Test Ban Treaty mentioned forty-four states by name that must ratify before entry into force.

8. For example, witness the power India exercised in blocking adoption of the Comprehensive Test Ban Treaty by the organization that initially negotiated it—the Conference on Disarmament, a body that acts exclusively on consensus. The treaty was eventually adopted in the UN General Assembly, which does not necessarily require a consensus.

9. *The Agency's Safeguards System (1965, as Provisionally Extended in 1966 and 1968)* (IAEA document INFCIRC/66/Rev. 2), September 16, 1968. Available online (www.iaea.org/worldatom/Documents/Infcircs/Others/inf66r2.shtml).

10. INFCIRC/540, Foreword, paras. 3, 4.

11. Pellaud and Hooper, "IAEA Safeguards in the 1990s."

12. See *The Structure and Content of Agreements between the Agency and States Required in Connection with the Treaty on the Non-Proliferation of Nuclear Weapons* (IAEA document INFCIRC/153 [Corrected], June 1972), article 116. Available online (www.iaea.org/worldatom/Documents/Infcircs/Others/inf153.shtml).

13. According to the Additional Protocol, "Nuclear fuel cycle–related research and development activities" means those activities specifically related to any process or system-development aspect of the following: conversion or enrichment of nuclear material; nuclear fuel fabrication; reactors; critical facilities; reprocessing of nuclear fuel; and processing of intermediate- or high-level waste containing plutonium, highly enriched uranium, or uranium-233. See INFCIRC/540, p. 14, Article 18.

14. Pellaud and Hooper, "IAEA Safeguards in the 1990s."

Chapter 3

Iran's Nuclear Policy and Program 93+2

Iran has been a signatory to the NPT since 1970 and has had a full-scope safeguards agreement with the IAEA since 1974 (INFCIRC/214 based on INFCIRC/153, the model full-scope safeguards agreement). The country has placed the Research Reactor 1 (TRR) in Tehran under IAEA safeguards, along with the Heavy-Water Zero-Power Reactor 1 (HWZPR), the Miniature Neutron Source Reactor 1 (MNSR), and the Light-Water Subcritical Reactor (LWSCR) in Esfahan.[1] Other nuclear facilities, including one subcritical nuclear reactor and one fuel-fabrication laboratory in Esfahan, nuclear research activities in Bonab and Ramsar, and laboratory-scale hot cells at Sharif University in Tehran, do not fall under IAEA safeguards because Iran has not declared them as containing nuclear materials.

In 1991, in an effort to dispel recurring suspicions about Iran's nuclear program, then-Director of the Atomic Energy Organization of Iran (AEOI) Reza Amrollahi stated that, in addition to permitting routine IAEA inspections of Iran's declared nuclear material, Iranian officials would agree to allow the IAEA to visit any location within Iran to verify the absence of undeclared nuclear activities.[2]

The agency has since made four such special visits. The first two were provoked by information transferred to the IAEA by the United States, while the last two visits were conducted in order to evaluate several sites that IAEA safeguards do not cover.[3] These trips were considered "visits" rather than special inspections (or even routine inspections) because the places and procedures were previously agreed upon and did not include all IAEA standard inspection measures.[4]

The first such instance occurred in February 1992, when the IAEA visited several locations that were not on Iran's list of declared nuclear sites:

> [T]he IAEA visited six locations, including Bushehr, the Esfahan Nuclear Technology Center, the Amirabad Nuclear Research Center in Tehran, the Karaj Agricultural and Medical Research Center, Saghand, and Moallem Kalayeh. . . . Of the six facilities, three had never previously been visited by the IAEA. Following the inspection, IAEA Deputy Director Jon Jennekens stated, 'We visited without any restriction everything we had asked to see. All nuclear activities in Iran are solely for peaceful purposes.' Regarding accusations that the IAEA had been led to a phony location and not to the real Moallem Kalayeh facility, David Kyd, a spokesman for the IAEA, stated, 'None of our member states ever suggested that we were taken to a wrong location.'[5]

In a press release published by the IAEA following the visit, the agency noted:

> The activities reviewed by the Team at the above-mentioned facilities and sites were found to be consistent with the peaceful application of nuclear energy and ionizing radiation. It should be clear that the Team's conclusions are limited to facilities and sites visited by it and are of relevance only to the time of the Team's visit.[6]

In a November 1993 follow-up visit, IAEA officials viewed facilities in Esfahan, Karaj, and Tehran.[7] This visit was also conducted on the basis of information provided by the United States and gathered inter alia from a Baghdad-based Iranian opposition group called the People's Mojahedin.[8] After visiting facilities in these three locations, the IAEA could not confirm any of the opposition group's claims. IAEA spokesman David Kyd announced that IAEA deputy director general for safeguards Bruno Pellaud (who succeeded Jennekens) "found no evidence . . . inconsistent with Iran's declaration that all its nuclear activities are peaceful."[9]

Following the visits in February 1992 and November 1993, the IAEA restated that it had found Iran to be in good standing with the NPT. The outcome of the visits did not allay U.S. concerns, however.[10] The U.S. response to the visits took two forms. Unofficially, "some sources claimed that the IAEA had been duped into visiting the wrong places despite a careful briefing from U.S. intelligence immediately before"[11]; these allegations could not be refuted or confirmed because of the IAEA's refusal to use Global Positioning System technology during its visits. Officially, however, the U.S. government "stopped referring to the visited sites in its public discussions of the alleged programme."[12]

At the same time, "Iran, understanding that the IAEA uses U.S. intelligence data, has kept the invitation open and allowed foreign journalists and non-government organizations to visit all of the sites visited by the IAEA."[13] The standing Iranian invitation has also encouraged a dialogue between several nonproliferation-oriented nongovernmental organizations and Iran. A delegation from the Federation of American Scientists later visited these sites; they found no activities inconsistent with peaceful nuclear uses, although they did not use all of the methods that the IAEA employs in its formal inspections.[14]

The third IAEA visit took place in July 1997, conducted by then–Director General of the IAEA Hans Blix. Prior to the visit, the AEOI had agreed that Blix would inspect two new research centers, one in Bonab and the other at Ramsar. After the visit, IAEA officials stated, "The IAEA ha[s] no information indicating any unreported activity at either site that is not in conformance with INFCIRC/214, Iran's safeguards agreement with the IAEA."[15]

The last visit, in May 2000, was carried out by Mohamed ElBaradei, the current IAEA director general, who visited the Bushehr nuclear power plant in southern Iran (INFCIRC/153 safeguards have not yet been applied to Bushehr because it is still under construction and thus does not contain safeguarded nuclear materials). Following his visit, ElBaradei was quoted by Iranian state radio as stating that Iran's nuclear program was peaceful and in conformity with international regulations.[16]

Safeguards Measures under Part I of Program 93+2

Part I of Program 93+2 was adopted in 1995 by the IAEA as measures previously extant but not implemented, and the agency has, since then, gradually implemented these measures as part of the existing safeguards agreement in all INFCIRC/153 states (for a detailed list of the measures adopted by the IAEA under each part of Program 93+2, see appendix 2). Implementation, however, is conditional upon states individually incorporating the provisions of Part I into their own safeguards agreement.

According to the most recent IAEA Safeguards Implementation Report, Iran is the only state that has yet to incorporate these provisions. Iran is expected to fully adopt Part I in 2002, and if it does, it will be required to submit an expanded declaration.[17] The following additional measures may be implemented by the IAEA under Part I: expanded access rights; expanded use of no-notice inspections; the right to perform special inspections; the use of improved verification techniques; and the right to receive national intelligence reports.

Expanded declaration. The expanded declaration includes not only the single document that states are presently required to submit under INFCIRC/153, but also an integration of additional information gathered by the agency regarding the state system of accounting and control (SSAC), nuclear material, facility operation and design, and broad descriptions of the state's nuclear program. The provision of expanded information, especially data about new nuclear installations well in advance of their start-up, is necessary in order to plan the most adequate measures for each facility.[18]

In short, the expanded declaration covers three categories:

1. Information on the SSAC that will enable the agency to improve the planning and efficiency of safeguards activities.
2. Information on present nuclear activities not routinely provided in the past: for example, the nature, purpose, location, and design of nuclear facilities and "locations-outside-facility" closed or decommissioned prior to the entry into force of the safeguards agreement; historical accounting and operating records prior to entry into force; descriptions of the nuclear

fuel cycle and other activities involving nuclear material, including a list of sites and nuclear-material-flow diagrams; and a description of nuclear-fuel-cycle-related research and development.

3. Information on planned nuclear activities, including design information for planned nuclear facilities and locations-outside-facility, as well as planned modifications of existing facilities that fall under the scope of INFCIRC/153.[19]

Expanded access rights. Expanded access can be obtained by collecting "location-specific" environmental samples at sites to which inspectors already have access. Through environmental sampling, the IAEA can identify the isotopic signatures of specific nuclear activities. Typical environmental samplings are swipe samples from inside and outside declared enrichment plants and hot-cell facilities, vegetation and soil samples, and hydrological samples (samples of grab high-volume water, sediments, and biota) for detecting undeclared high enrichment of uranium and plutonium separation.

The location-specific monitoring samples approved under Part I of Program 93+2 are sent for analysis to the new IAEA clean laboratory at Seibersdorf, Austria. For a more accurate and sophisticated (but also lengthy and expensive) process called "particle analysis," the samples are sent abroad to more specialized laboratories. Currently, the collection and evaluation of high-volume air samples, approved only under Part II of the program, are not foreseen.[20]

Expanded use of unannounced (no-notice) routine inspections at strategic points within nuclear facilities and sites. A no-notice inspection requires "no advance notification regarding [its] timing, activities, or locations. . . . In practice this means that the state is informed of the IAEA's intention to perform such an inspection when its inspector arrives at the entrance to the site in question."[21] IAEA inspectors can arrive at the entrance of a site at any time, although access to the facility may be delayed up to two hours. No-notice inspections may be carried out in order to verify flows of nuclear material at large facilities; confirm the status of decommissioned facilities and facilities under construction; certify the nonoperating status of nuclear facilities; and confirm that facilities are not being used for clandestine purposes (e.g., unreported irradiation at reactors or the production of highly enriched uranium at enrichment plants).

Nevertheless, there are some limitations to no-notice inspections: (1) in states in which arriving foreigners are checked at the airport, the authorities immediately know of the inspectors' arrival and therefore have enough time to prepare for the inspection; (2) no-notice inspections are limited to strategic points within routine inspections; (3) the use of a no-notice inspection during ad hoc, special, and design-information verifications is not permitted; and (4) the use of no-notice inspections is generally limited to "those situations where environmental sampling techniques or unattended surveillance devices could not be effectively used."[22]

The right to carry out special inspections either at strategic points within a facility or at other locations in which the state has declared the presence of nuclear material. Special inspections at strategic points may be conducted only to confirm that all nuclear material required to be under safeguards has been reported to the IAEA. In other words, if all material in a declared site is under safeguards, a special inspection can verify that diversion has not taken place.

As became evident in the case of Iraq, however, inspections at strategic points do not provide the ability to detect activity taking place in undeclared rooms or sites if the activity does not intersect with declared material.

Application of improved verification techniques. Improved verification measures and tools include swipe tests, remote control, digital cameras, and electronic seals.

The right of the IAEA to receive national intelligence reports that could facilitate the performance of its mission. The IAEA can compare these reports to a state's declaration and incorporate information contained in the reports into the agency's internal records (safeguards inspection data and information received on the import and export of nuclear material). In addition, other resources can be used by the IAEA in evaluating intelligence reports, such as information from the agency's own databases on open resources (e.g., media reports and scientific publications); on states' nuclear regulations; on power and research reactors; and on companies, firms, and organizations working in the nuclear field.[23]

Safeguards Measures under Part II of Program 93+2

Part II of Program 93+2 (the Additional Protocol) contains measures that do not fall under the legal mandate of the IAEA; therefore, every state is required to approve it unilaterally. Because Iran has refused to adopt the Additional Protocol, the following IAEA activities, although approved under Part II, fall outside of the agency's permitted activities in Iran:

- Receiving information about and access to all nuclear-fuel-cycle-related locations and activities, from mines to waste storage (according to INFCIRC/153, nuclear material containing uranium or thorium that "has not been processed to a suitable stage for fuel fabrication or enrichment" is not subject to safeguards[24]), and to any other locations containing nuclear material intended for nonnuclear uses.

- Receiving information about and access to all buildings on a nuclear site, even if they do not contain nuclear materials. The IAEA will be entitled, when expanded access is permitted, to carry out such specified activities as visual observation, environmental sampling, radiation monitoring and measuring, and sealing.
- Receiving information about, and inspection mechanisms for, fuel-cycle-related research and development activities even if nuclear materials are not present.
- Receiving information about the manufacturing and export of sensitive, nuclear-related technologies.
- Collecting environmental samples of air, water, vegetation, soil, and smears beyond declared locations or over wide areas.
- Conducting no-notice inspections at a nuclear facility or location-outside-facility during a "design information verification" visit.

To Adhere or Not to Adhere

Iranian officials and the AEOI have repeatedly rejected accusations that Iran is carrying out any nonpeaceful nuclear programs or activities. But following approval of the Additional Protocol by the IAEA's board of governors, political pressure on Iran to adopt the protocol began to mount. The Iranian government has resisted this pressure, citing several reasons behind its refusal to sign.

First, Iran has stated that it will not adopt the protocol as long as it is denied civilian nuclear technology for its civilian nuclear program, especially for Bushehr. Iran insists on exercising its right under Article IV of the NPT to obtain peaceful nuclear technology without interference from the United States or any other country.[25]

Second, Iran has stated that the protocol "should be applied equally and in a nondiscriminatory manner to nuclear facilities and activities of all state members of the agency, in particular nuclear weapons states."[26] It should be noted that inspection of NWS facilities for diversion is purely symbolic. Although all five NWSs have voluntarily signed—but not yet ratified—the Additional Protocol, it covers only their civilian nuclear programs, not their nuclear weapons programs, and even those agreements are limited. For example, the U.S. agreement includes a provision that allows it to restrict IAEA inspections within its civilian facilities for national security reasons.[27]

Third, Iran has described as unsatisfactory the manner in which the universality of the Additional Protocol was determined,[28] declaring that it would accept Program 93+2 safeguards only if adopted more widely.[29] Specifically, Iran has mentioned that Israel's refusal to accept full-scope safeguards on all of its nuclear activities "might make implementation of the protocol problematic."[30] Iranian leaders—paraphrasing an Israeli statement on Israel's own policy—have said that Iran would not be the first country in the Middle East to adopt the Additional Protocol, nor would it be the last.[31] As of May 2002, Jordan is the only Middle Eastern state that has adopted the protocol.

Finally, Iran has cited concerns about the Additional Protocol itself. According to Iranian officials, "the large volume of information to be supplied by signatories to the protocol would increase the administrative burden on member states." Moreover, they expressed concern that the IAEA secretariat "should remain independent and impartial, not in any way using the protocol as a political tool in favour of some member states against others."[32]

Because the pressure on Iran to adopt the Additional Protocol will continue, it is important to examine the country's policy toward the protocol under two possible scenarios: (1) Iran decides not to develop nuclear weapons and fully complies with its arms control obligations; (2) Iran takes steps toward the development of a clandestine nuclear program.

As in other states, Iran's decisionmaking process with regard to nuclear policy is a product of relationships among multiple actors. First, it is unclear who is ultimately responsible for the state's nuclear activities. The AEOI is probably responsible for the civilian nuclear program, while the Islamic Revolutionary Guard Corps "is believed to be in charge of Iran's chemical, biological, and nuclear weapons programs, and its operational chemical and biological weapons inventories and missile forces."[33]

Second, similar to other states that have faced the decision of whether or not to pursue a nuclear option, Iran is undergoing an internal debate between hardliners and reformists. Whereas the latter group are of the opinion that Iran should join and observe the international arms control system, hardliners advocate the development of independent, indigenous Iranian nuclear weapons capabilities. Iran's rationale for signing major arms control treaties and cooperating with the IAEA inspections regime should be understood in light of this internal power struggle, including the reformists' desire for Iran to retain international respectability.[34]

Scenario 1: Iran in Full Compliance with Its Nonproliferation Obligations

Should Iran decide to comply fully with its nonproliferation obligations, it would probably (like any other country) adopt the Additional Protocol in such a way and at such a time as to maximize political, economic, and technological gains while minimizing costs. In the short run, it would seem that Iran has neither an incentive to adopt the protocol nor a disincentive to continue rejecting it.

One reason for this current Iranian policy is the limited adoption of the Additional Protocol by other IAEA member states. As of May 2002, of the sixty-two states who had signed the protocol, only twenty-five had ratified it (see appendix 3). As mentioned previously, Jordan is the only adopting Middle Eastern state.

Such limited participation can be explained partly by the added burden that the protocol places on states, especially those with significant nuclear activities—that is, the burden of applying domestic regulations as well as adapting facilities to meet the protocol requirements. As of May 2002, Canada and Japan were the only states with significant nuclear activities that had signed and ratified the protocol. States with minor nuclear activities (or none at all) have displayed a similar lack of urgency to join. Once more states with significant nuclear programs join, their membership will strengthen the perception of the Additional Protocol as the nonproliferation norm and legitimize the application of political pressure on states that have not yet adopted it.

But as long as the limited response of signatories persists and INFCIRC/153, in the interim, continues to serve as the de facto safeguards agreement for most states, Iran will find little reason to adopt the Additional Protocol. Indeed, the country can be considered in good standing and in full compliance with its NPT obligations without doing so. Only when the number of ratifying states increases significantly—recognizing that the protocol will be effective only if widely adopted—will the diplomatic as well as technological pressure on Iran increase, and its refusal to join become even more of a significant international issue.

Another reason for Iran's reluctance to adopt the protocol is that it may prefer to keep its options open. Indeed, even if Iran does not intend to develop nuclear weapons, an ambiguous nuclear policy might strengthen the country's role as a leader in the region. Yet, the political, technical, and (probably) economic restrictions of an ambiguous nuclear policy will likely outweigh any gains in the long run. Thus, Iran, in weighing whether or not to adopt the protocol, will use delaying tactics until it can ensure that by joining it will maximize its gains, such as achieving the legitimacy it seeks from the international community, not least to facilitate the importing of technology, equipment, and materials to support its civilian nuclear energy program.

Ukraine's decision to surrender its nuclear weapons capabilities in exchange for financial compensation, technical assistance, and national security guarantees provides an example of how security and economic concerns can be addressed successfully in exchange for nuclear rollback. Success in dissuading Iran through such incentives, however, will be relevant only if Iran makes the strategic decision not to develop a nuclear weapons option.

Scenario 2: Iran Takes Steps toward Developing a Nuclear Weapons Program

The second scenario is based on the assumption that Iran decides to develop a nuclear weapons program. An NNWS can take any of five paths to acquire such a program: diversion, bypass, parallel program, breakout, and legal.[35]

The Diversion Path. Under this path, a state secretly diverts nuclear material from its safeguarded civil nuclear program and uses it for its clandestine nuclear weapons program. Preventing the diversion of technology supplied by the IAEA or by industrialized states was the main focus of IAEA founders in 1957, and INFCIRC/153 was designed primarily to prevent states from utilizing this option—specifically, to expose diversion of a "significant quantity"[36] from declared facilities.

If Iran remains a signatory only to INFCIRC/153 it could risk pursuing this option, relying on the fact that safeguards inspections take place at agreed-upon times and places. As in Iraq's own crash program (which it developed while under the INFCIRC/153 agreement), Iran could conduct research and still be in compliance with IAEA safeguards. Essentially, it could divert fissile material the day after an inspection takes place and then proceed to operate in some sites six months to a year without the diversion being discovered. With the addition of Part I of Program 93+2 as an integral component of the INFCIRC/153 agreement, this might be a risk Iran would be more reluctant to take. However, since Iran has not yet incorporated Part I measures into its safeguards agreement, the IAEA is limited to the same safeguards measures that applied to Iraq before the Gulf War.

The Bypass Path. Under this path, nuclear material is clandestinely introduced into a country's civil program (for enriching, irradiating, or reprocessing) through the circumvention of safeguards, and is then removed from the declared site. This possibility is addressed only partially by INFCIRC/153 and the Additional Protocol. The perceived risk inherent in this path is lower than that of the diversion path. The violating state relies on the probability that the IAEA will be unable to discern that undeclared materials entered the civil facility, were worked on, and were subsequently removed. Although it is difficult to prove that undeclared activities have taken place at a given site, Iran may not be willing to take this risk, especially given the IAEA's success in ultimately detecting such activity in North Korea.

The North Korean case is important from a verification as well as a nonproliferation perspective. In the early 1990s, North Korea maintained a pilot reprocessing plant that was not fully operational but still capable of separating gram quantities of plutonium,[37] a capability not included in the initial report that Pyongyang presented to the IAEA in May 1992. The plant had not been placed under safeguards in part because no declaration had been made that the plant contained nuclear materials. Because the IAEA had access to national technical means—previously used only in the Iraqi case—the agency was able to detect the introduction of the undeclared material. This case also highlights the importance of applying IAEA safeguards to sites that allegedly remain under construction (e.g., Bushehr), as well as to decommissioned facilities.

The Parallel Program Path. Under this path, a state creates a clandestine nuclear weapons program parallel to its safeguarded civil program, with no intersection between the two. As became clear from the Iraqi experience, the adoption of some instrument—such as that provided by the Additional Protocol—is needed to preclude such a development. If Iran chooses to exercise the parallel program option, it would probably not adopt (or would at least sign without ratifying) the Additional Protocol, thus remaining under INFCIRC/153, which lacks the more intrusive measures needed to expose a parallel nuclear program.

The Breakout Path. Under this path, a state openly violates its obligation not to acquire or develop nuclear weapons. This scenario would likely come into play if Iran perceives that threats to its national security outweigh the potential international response to such a violation. In such a case, Iran would probably announce that it had developed a nuclear weapon (or exhibit obvious signs to that effect), whether or not it actually possessed such a weapon. Short of such a declaration, Iran would risk preemptive action as well as political, economic, and possibly international military responses if it were found to have a nascent nuclear weapons program.

Factors that might cause Iran to risk the breakout path include Iraqi acceleration of its WMD program, an intensified posture by U.S. troops in the Persian Gulf or other Arab states, an escalation of turmoil across the Iranian border in Central Asia, or an augmentation of threats to Iran's hegemony in the region. Unless such a threat is imminent, however, Iran could choose the next option, the legal path, to achieve the same goals at a much lower cost.

The Legal Path. In accordance with NPT withdrawal provisions, a state can withdraw from the treaty with three months' notice if it can demonstrate that "extraordinary events, related to the subject matter of the treaty, have jeopardized its supreme interests."[38] Because this condition is so vague, it is not difficult to imagine specific examples of an "extraordinary event" that Iran might present to justify its withdrawal.[39] Indeed, Ali Rafsanjani, then-speaker of the Iranian parliament, stated in 1988, "[the Iran-Iraq War] taught us that international laws are only scraps of paper. . . . [T]he world does not respect its own resolutions and closes its eyes to the violations and all the aggressions. . . ."[40]

Although any sovereign country has the right to withdraw from a treaty, no state has exercised that right before with regard to the NPT; even North Korea reversed its threat to withdraw at the last minute. Nevertheless, one risk extant under the NPT withdrawal clause is that a state will build up a nuclear program and then—possessing either the bomb or the expertise to build one—withdraw.

As in the first scenario, as long as the Additional Protocol continues to be adopted by a limited number of states, Iran will avoid taking any steps toward adoption that might expose a clandestine program (e.g., giving the IAEA supplementary verification rights). In the long run, the risk of exposure for Iran, should it adopt the Additional Protocol, would be high because the IAEA would likely employ highly elaborate and intrusive measures not used in the country previously. It is not clear whether Iran would be willing to take this kind of risk.

But a decision by Iran to stay outside the international nonproliferation norm would raise even more suspicions about the country's objectives and would encourage states to use national technical means, if not preemptive action, to deter Iranian proliferation. Assuming that Iran therefore chooses to develop its nuclear weapons program clandestinely, it will have to use deception and denial techniques to conceal it.

Deception "involves the use of active or passive measures to convey a false or inaccurate picture of a clandestine activity" (e.g., disguising a nuclear weapons production facility inside a military base), while denial "entails the use of active measures (camouflage, electronic emission control, and various forms of physical, personnel, and communications security) to conceal the very existence of a clandestine program."[41] When the intended target of the deception, in this case the IAEA, receives false signals, it too plays a part in the process by unwittingly assembling these signals in such a way as to confirm the intended (false) picture.[42]

There are five main categories of deception and denial techniques that a state can employ to prevent its nuclear program from being exposed: political, legal, counterintelligence, procurement/acquisition, and safeguards. The more complex and large the program, the broader the range of techniques a state must use in order to conceal that program.

Political Techniques

Should Iran choose to develop nuclear weapons, one of the key decisions for Iranian officials would be whether or not to do so while overtly complying with the terms of the NPT. Such a strategy would deflect any undue attention from the clandestine program and thus minimize complications in Iran's procurement and development efforts.

For example, Saddam Husayn once asked Jaffar Dhia Jaffar, the eventual scientific head of the Iraqi nuclear program, whether that program would be hindered in any way if Iraq remained in the NPT. Jaffar's answer was "an immediate and unequivocal no: . . . it would have absolutely no effect upon Iraq's program."[43] Indeed, throughout the 1980s, Iraq played an active role in the IAEA's various programs, welcomed agency staff to its al-Tuwaitha Nuclear Research Center, sought and received technical assistance, and was a frequent member of the agency's board of governors. Iraq repeatedly emphasized the peaceful and safeguarded nature of its nuclear facilities and contrasted its openness to inspection with Israel's refusal to sign the NPT.[44]

It is easy to see how Iran could employ similar methods. Nevertheless, the more relaxed verification regime of the 1980s and 1990s no longer holds. If Iran were to adopt the Additional Protocol and develop a clandestine program, it would do so today with less confidence that this program would remain undetected.

Although the Additional Protocol cannot prevent a state from developing nuclear weapons, it does put up certain barriers. Under the more restricted verification regime of the Additional Protocol, a state that decides to develop a clandestine nuclear weapons program must invest many more resources to that end than it would otherwise, including time, manpower, money, and sophistication.

Iran's policy toward another international arms control initiative—the Chemical Weapons Convention—may shed some light on the country's future political approach to the Additional Protocol. Most scholars in the field assumed that Iran would not sign the CWC; that if it did, it would not ratify the treaty; and that if it did ratify, it definitely would not submit the required stockpile declaration.[45] These assumptions were proven incorrect. Iran indeed signed and ratified the CWC and then submitted the required stockpile declaration to the Organization for the Prohibition of Chemical Weapons (OPCW), the organization charged with verifying CWC compliance.

Yet, Iran has likely possessed chemical weapons since 1988 and made limited use of them in response to Iraqi chemical attacks during the Iran-Iraq War.[46] In November 1998, Iranian ambassador Mohammad R. Alborzi, in his address to the Conference of the States Parties to the Chemical Weapons Convention, stated:

> the decision was made that, on a strictly limited scale capabilities should be developed to challenge the imminent threat particularly against the civilian populated centers. We declared, at the time, that Iran had chemical weapons capability, while maintaining the policy not to resort to these weapons and rely on diplomacy as the sole mechanism to stop their use by its adversary. . . . Following the establishment of cease-fire, the decision to develop chemical weapons capabilities was reversed and the process was terminated. It was reiterated consequently that Iran would not seek or produce chemical weapons and would accelerate its efforts to ensure early conclusion of a comprehensive and total ban under the CWC. This has continued to be my government's policy ever since.[47]

Many Western policymakers and scholars, however, dispute Iran's claims that it has both terminated its chemical weapons program and destroyed its chemical weapons stockpiles. According to a 2001 CIA report, Iran "has manufactured and stockpiled chemical weapons, including blister, blood, choking, and probably nerve agents, and the bombs and artillery shells to deliver them."[48]

Despite lingering suspicions, Iran's declaration to the OPCW has not yet been subject to a challenge inspection, a permissible technique under the terms of the CWC for verifying a state's declaration; the OPCW is concerned about the impact that a failed challenge inspection (i.e., an inspection that does not reveal any evidence of chemical weapons) could have on its credibility.

Iran's strategy with regard to nuclear weapons, however, is different. Since the general belief is that Iran already possesses chemical weapons, the risk of exposure with regard to those weapons would not rival the impact of a revelation that the country possesses a nuclear option. The working assumption of Western intelligence agencies is that Iran does not yet possess that option. Current estimates suggest that, if Iran could not obtain fissile material from other sources, it would need five to seven years to develop a nuclear bomb. In recent testimony before the Senate Select Committee on Intelligence, CIA director George Tenet assessed that "Tehran may be able to indigenously produce enough fissile material for a nuclear weapon by late this decade. Obtaining material from outside could cut years from this estimate."[49]

As long as Iran remains under the current limited safeguards regime, the IAEA will continue to verify only declared sites and only nuclear materials at strategic points within those sites. Moreover, since Iran has not yet incorporated Part I of Program 93+2 into its safeguards agreement, it could use techniques similar to those used by Iraq to avoid detection. The IAEA has recently faced the same problem in another Middle Eastern state, Algeria.

Algeria joined the NPT in 1995 but has been under partial IAEA safeguards (INFCIRC/66) since 1992 as part of a reactor-supply deal, enabling the IAEA to inspect specific, agreed-upon buildings within a nuclear site near the city of Ain Oussera. Although Algeria has permitted the

IAEA to inspect this site since 1992, it has not allowed the agency "to inspect all of the facilities at the site, some of which are at the very center of the controversy over potential plutonium production." Moreover, European and Arab governments "continue to express concern [that] Algeria's nuclear program seems too extensive for civilian needs."[50]

Because Algeria has not yet adopted the Additional Protocol, the IAEA has the authority to inspect only the declared buildings—strictly speaking, only the rooms declared by Algerian officials as containing nuclear materials. If Algeria were to agree to adopt the protocol, "the IAEA would have the authority to inspect all the buildings at the site."[51] Even then, however, the agency's verification efforts would remain limited in certain respects, as some of the suspect buildings are facilities adjacent to, not inside, the site. Because those buildings are as yet undeclared, and the IAEA has no proof that they contain nuclear materials, the agency—under the terms of the Additional Protocol—could examine them only with a special inspections permit.

The IAEA has been reluctant to request special inspections in the past, primarily out of a desire to avoid political embarrassment for state members and to prevent questions from arising about the reliability and effectiveness of the safeguards system itself. Moreover, although the president of the UNSC issued a 1992 statement declaring that "the SC would regard any proliferation of WMD as a threat to international peace and security, and its members would take appropriate action on any violation reported by the IAEA,"[52] this commitment lost some of its credibility when the IAEA's first and only request to exercise its special inspection rights (in order to verify North Korea's declaration) was blocked in the UNSC by China.

Legal Techniques

As long as the security balance in the Middle East is not altered in a way that would increase Iran's threat perception, the option of signing but not ratifying the protocol may be the most practical one in the eyes of the Iranian government, should it choose to develop a nuclear weapons program.

When a state adopts an international agreement, it does so in two stages. The first stage consists of the signature: by signing a treaty, a state indicates its intent to become a party to that treaty, and it obliges itself to refrain from acts that would defeat the treaty's object and purpose. Although a signature often represents the first step in becoming a state party, it does not establish consent to be bound by the terms of the treaty.[53]

The second stage is ratification. By ratifying a treaty, a state expresses its definitive consent to be legally bound by the treaty's terms.[54] The ratification process itself has two dimensions: an international component involving deposit of the legal ratification agreement with the IAEA, and a domestic component in which a state's domestic legislation is brought into compliance with the agreement.

For instance, after a treaty is signed by the United States, the president must submit the treaty to the Senate; the Senate then refers it to the Senate Foreign Relations Committee, which generally conducts hearings and makes a recommendation to the full Senate. Finally, the Senate must pass a resolution of advice and consent to the ratification of the treaty by a two-thirds quorum vote (a constitutional requirement), and only then is the president entitled to formally ratify the treaty.[55]

The entry into force of the Additional Protocol for each state is either the date that the IAEA receives notification from the state that the statutory and constitutional requirements for entry into force have been met, or upon signature by the state's representatives and the IAEA. The state chooses one of the two alternatives according to its own internal legal requirements.[56]

By signing the Additional Protocol but not ratifying it, Iran would secure the benefits of a signatory and be considered a party in good faith without being obliged to the protocol legally or technically. The IAEA and the international community, however, would have limited verification and enforcement capability to ensure Iranian compliance; in fact, until Iran incorporates Part I of Program 93+2 into its safeguards agreement, its de facto safeguards obligations will remain limited to INFCIRC/153—placing Iran in the same legal situation under which Iraq was able to develop its clandestine nuclear weapons program. The IAEA will have to work within these constraints unless it takes advantage of the "open invitation" issued by Iranian officials in 1991 or requests permission to conduct a special inspection.

Signing the protocol while delaying ratification might also serve as an important step toward removing the suspicion surrounding Iran's nuclear activities. Russia and certain other states are waiting anxiously for Iran to acquire the slightest legitimacy with regard to its nuclear program so that economic and technical cooperation efforts with Tehran can be intensified. As of now, Russian-Iranian cooperation has been limited by the economic and political pressure (and sometimes sanctions) that the United States places on entities suspected of cooperating in prohibited activities with Iran. Iran's signature, even without ratification, could be used by Russia as a pretense to insist that the Iranian nuclear program is being used only for peaceful purposes and that any cooperation offered by Russia toward the development of that program is therefore legitimate.[57]

In the long run, by not signing the protocol, Iran would jeopardize its access to foreign technology. The country's credibility and legitimacy with regard to its avowals of peaceful intent would also be damaged, bringing to a halt any possibility of open cooperation from the West.

Alternately, by signing the protocol but delaying ratification, Iran would achieve political benefits and probably even technological cooperation, since states would assume that Iran's adoption of the protocol was forthcoming. Should it choose this option, Iran could also exhaust political, diplomatic, and economic tradeoffs for ratification. Iran has even mentioned "a procedural obstacle" it might use in the future to delay ratification: arguing that some Additional Protocol provisions might conflict with the country's national regulations—that is, "implementation might prove to be difficult" if Iran cannot "reconcile national legislation with the protocol's provisions."[58]

Should Iran choose to develop a nuclear weapons program, its decision to implement this strategy—to sign and avoid ratification of the protocol—would take place only after it had an estimate of the time needed to complete the program (probably after it begins to produce fissile material or succeeds in obtaining a sufficient amount from other sources). It would also need time to assure that it had all the technical means needed for the production and assembly of nuclear weapons and that no major obstacles remained that could affect the program. In addition, it would want to be in possession of all source and process materials to avoid being adversely affected by sanctions, boycotts, or other possible outside interference.

Counterintelligence Techniques

The use of intelligence channels to pass false signals is a common deception technique, since intelligence plays a key role in guiding inspectors to suspicious sites. Although the IAEA has a department responsible for collecting open data, it does not have an intelligence unit. Intelligence is gathered mostly by IAEA member states, which must consider the risks of compromising sources and methods in determining which information, if any, to share with the agency. Relevant intelligence can be gathered via "satellite photographs, line drawings derived from overhead imagery, defector reports, and information on [isotopic] 'signatures,' or indicators of illicit weapons activity."[59]

Iraq effectively used counterintelligence to both conceal and create a false picture about its nuclear program. The Iraqi intelligence services placed inspectors under intensive surveillance, bugging their hotel rooms, conference rooms, and office spaces, and monitoring their radio frequencies and telephone conversations. In addition, a number of Iraqi spies were planted in UNSCOM's Baghdad field organization. As a result, several no-notice inspections were compromised beforehand, permitting the Iraqis to remove any trace of nuclear activity.[60]

The Iraqis developed other deception techniques by studying the monitoring methods employed by the IAEA and Western intelligence agencies and then attempting to counter them. For example, the United States shared satellite imagery with Iraq throughout the 1980s during the Iran-Iraq War. Iraqi counterintelligence officials thereby acquired familiarity with the capabilities of U.S. reconnaissance satellites, including the technical limitations of those satellites and the ways in which their data was analyzed. Putting this knowledge to use, Baghdad has gone to great lengths to conceal many of its key nuclear weapons facilities from Western intelligence agencies.[61]

A serious problem afflicting Western intelligence on Iraq has been "mirror-imaging," a term that describes the tendency to see one's adversary as behaving according to one's own logic and values. Iraqi counterintelligence officials have used this natural propensity in order to "exploit deep-seated misconceptions and prejudices on the part of Western intelligence analysts," who often assume "that other countries use the same production technologies and safety and environmental standards as those employed in the West."[62]

For example, it took IAEA inspectors several visits to realize that a somewhat squalid, rundown site they thought was being used for industrial purposes was in fact one of Iraq's main nuclear weapons sites. The confusion lay in the site's loose safety standards; the mirror-imaging tendency evident in this case was demonstrated in a statement made by one of the American inspectors, who claimed that the site could not be a nuclear weapons site because "you cannot work with radioactive material in the spaces they have designed and meet the latest [U.S. Occupational Safety and Health Administration] standards."[63] Needless to say, it is unlikely that the Iraqis were particularly concerned about U.S. workplace standards.

In another Iraqi case, a first inspection revealed a major weapons testing bunker. Several of the inspectors argued that the bunker "couldn't be the real site, because there [were] not enough data collectors and data streams coming off [it]."[64] The reality was that this site was built on the model of old U.S. weapons development facilities (e.g., those used in the Manhattan Project), which the American inspectors were either too young to remember or had never seen before.

Procurement and Acquisition Techniques

The most important stage in the development of a nuclear program is the acquisition of fissile material (highly enriched uranium and plutonium). There are two methods by which a state can obtain this material: by enrichment or separation, or by buying it on the black market. Some suspect that Iran, like Iraq previously, is using both methods in order to expedite the development of nuclear weapons once its program reaches the stage at which fissile material is needed. For instance, some have argued that Iran has "several efforts under way to produce fissile material indigenously." Although Iran "would regard centrifuges as the most promising approach" to this goal, Iranian officials have "hedged their bets" by attempting to acquire "laser isotope enrichment technology from Russia" and "a heavy-water-moderated plutonium production reactor" from several different countries.[65]

The main obstacle facing a rogue state seeking to buy source materials is obvious: who will risk selling such destructive materials to a regime suspected of developing nuclear weapons? To counter this obstacle, a country may employ "a Byzantine procurement network involving multiple shell companies and transshipment points," all designed to "conceal its acquisition of sensitive technologies from abroad." Moreover, "[c]omponents for key factories and weapon systems [might be] imported from several suppliers or in unfinished form so that the intended military end-use would not be apparent."[66]

For example, to obtain its calutrons, Iraq bought large iron-pole magnets from a state-owned Austrian firm and shipped them to Iraq, half by truck through Turkey and half by ship through Hamburg. The Austrians did not question the purpose of the magnets, and the Iraqis, of course, did not volunteer the information. In another deception strategy, Iraq invested in legitimate foreign firms that either manufactured equipment useful to the Iraqi nuclear program or had the ability to legitimately order such equipment, ostensibly for the firms' own use.[67] In addition, when purchasing items sensitive to export controls, Iraq placed orders in quantities small enough to avoid triggering the controls established by the Nuclear Supplier Group (NSG).[68]

As a result of these experiences, NSG regulations were tightened to include dual-use equipment and materials. Today, it is the importer who is responsible for identifying the user and the uses of imports, while the exporting firm or its agents confirm those facts. Yet, companies seldom conduct onsite inspections before or after the sale of dual-use items. Thus, the actual destination of exported dual-use items or nuclear materials is rarely established with certainty.

Safeguards Techniques

The principal impediment to exposing undeclared nuclear activities is the difficulty in identifying "dual-capable facilities that could be used either for legitimate commercial activities or for illicit weapons purposes."[69] For example,

> Iraqi engineers devised several deception techniques to disguise the main EMIS [electromagnetic isotope separation] site at Tarmiya. The plant had no security fence or visible supply of electricity, suggesting to Western photointerpreters that it was of little strategic significance. Only after the war did UNSCOM inspectors discover that the Tarmiya facility was powered by a 30 kilovolt underground cable from a 150 megawatt substation several kilometers away. The EMIS plant was also situated within a large military security zone, so that it did not require any additional perimeter security or military defenses.[70]

Other safeguards techniques used by Iraq have included the duplication and dispersal of weapons-development and -production activities over a large number of sites, and the use of shifting code names for individual programs or sites.[71]

Another kind of deception was practiced by Iraq during the verification process itself. Iraqi officials demonstrated the advantage of hiding a clandestine program in plain sight when they chose al-Tuwaitha—the sole, declared Iraqi nuclear research site inspected by the IAEA—as the initial center of Iraq's clandestine nuclear program. Indeed, al-Tuwaitha was visited every six months by IAEA safeguards inspectors, along with two deputy directors general of the IAEA, many IAEA staff members, and Western scientists, all of whom indicated that they saw no suspicious activity. This openness was illusory, however. The Iraqis permitted IAEA inspectors to visit only declared sites—that is, only portions of three of the nearly one hundred buildings at al-Tuwaitha—while IAEA staff and Western scientists were guided through selected laboratories and forced to hold their meetings in the center's conference building. Although these restrictions on movement could have been viewed as a warning signal, they were not recognized as such at the time. The visitors were "managed" through busy schedules, generous hospitality, and cultural tourism.[72]

To fully understand the extent of the deception, one must look at the al-Tuwaitha site map (see next page). UN inspectors in Iraq did not see this map in its entirety until 1991, when it was presented to them by U.S. intelligence just before the IAEA Action Team's first special inspection. According to Dimitri Perricos, former deputy leader of the IAEA Action Team, "It was the first time that the IAEA was able to see the magnitude of the site"—a site that the agency had been visiting since before the Gulf War, twice a year for almost twenty years:

> To our surprise, Tuwaitha was a very, very large center. It was not just the three or four buildings that safeguards inspectors had visited before the war—the two reactors, a small storage facility, and a small laboratory-scale fabrication plant. We found that there was a whole new area of Tuwaitha where safeguards inspectors had never been before. This area was only known to those people who had access to aerial surveillance.

Al-Tuwaitha Site Map

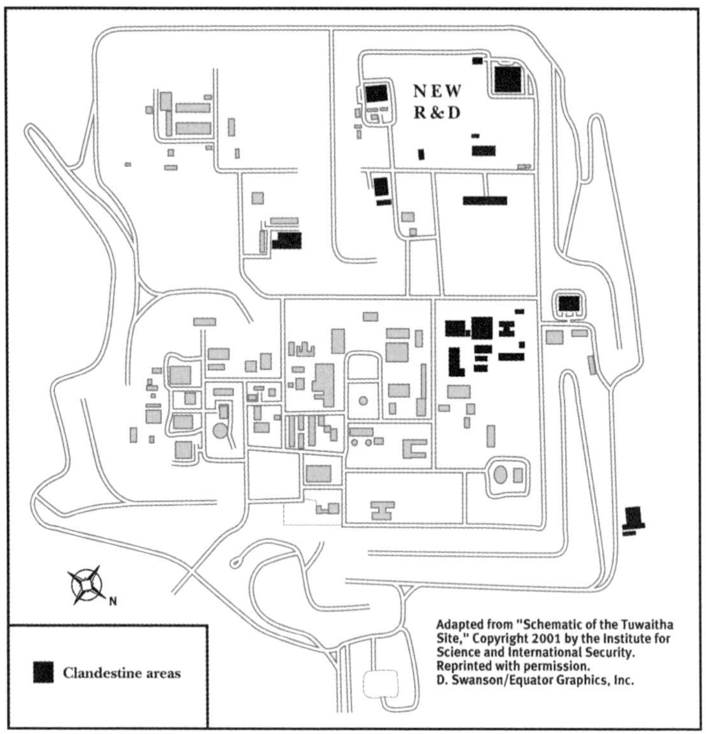

> It was in this area, called the new R&D area, where Iraq did most of its clandestine development work. . . .
>
> The Iraqis had constructed big berms, about 30 meters high, around the site. On top, they had anti-aircraft guns because, of course, of the Israeli bombing of the Tamuz reactor and for the defense of the site from Iranian aircraft. But at the same time, the berms were able to hide areas of the site from [the] eyes of visitors, including safeguards inspectors.[73]

Self-delusion undoubtedly played a part in some inspectors assessing a peaceful nature to al-Tuwaitha, but their false perception can also be attributed to Iraq's deft management of the inspection visits, as well as to the deliberately deceptive layout of the facility itself. The placement of the buildings, the visual screening provided by trees, and the careful routing of the internal road system made it difficult for visitors without access to satellite imagery to accurately gauge the size of the center and the articulation of the buildings.[74]

As long as Iran remains legally bound only by INFCIRC/153, having rejected the Additional Protocol, it could potentially use many of the same techniques practiced by Iraq in order to deceive inspectors. Indeed, most pre–Gulf War limitations on access and information governing inspectors in Iraq will remain in place in Iran unless the latter decides to adopt the protocol.

Conclusion

In signing but not ratifying the Additional Protocol, Iran could create a breathing space of at least several years while the protocol is adopted by other countries. These years would be critical to the development of an Iranian nuclear weapons program, especially if, by taking this step, Iran were to gain political as well as technological cooperation from other states, especially Russia. Within this "semi-adoption" (signature without ratification) status, Iran could continue to develop its nuclear capacity until it was forced to reveal the existence of its arsenal. At that point, it could employ either the "breakout" or "legal" paths described earlier.

Iran may decide to ratify the Additional Protocol in the future. If so, the IAEA's best opportunity to detect a clandestine nuclear weapons program would be an Iranian diversion of declared material that is under safeguards. If the IAEA were to discover a discrepancy that Iran could not resolve, the agency could initiate a special inspection or request expanded access to clarify the discrepancy.

In light of the bitter experience and lack of political support that the IAEA has suffered in the past, however, it may be reluctant to either request a special inspection or take Iran up on its "open invitation," especially after conducting four visits and finding nothing. Indeed, unless the IAEA has definitive information on undeclared materials or prohibited activity (a "smoking gun"), it is unlikely to resort to this sensitive, controversial measure too often, largely because of the embarrassment that a failure would cause.[75]

Special inspections also require a state's consent regarding time, location, and specific rooms to be inspected. Taking advantage of these restrictions, a state can utilize measures such as cleaning a suspected room prior to inspection in order to remove any sign of clandestine activity; if done carefully, this measure can diminish significantly the IAEA's inspections capacity in that room. The new measures under Part I, however, make such deception more difficult, and the risk of exposure much higher, by granting the IAEA powers to act more quickly and investigate the declared sites more thoroughly when a violation is discovered.

Indeed, the probability of discovering undeclared activities at sites in which inspections are already taking place is much better today, with Part I already in place, than prior to the Gulf War. The new measures, especially short-notice inspections and location-specific sampling, allow the agency much more intrusive means of identifying undeclared nuclear activities.

But Iran has not yet incorporated these measures, and even if it were to do so, the IAEA would have no automatic right to search undeclared locations—even those close to a declared site—without clear evidence of discrepancy.

Moreover, in a state as large as Iran, the problems inherent in exposing undeclared nuclear activities are particularly daunting. The IAEA cannot blindly search a state for undeclared activity. Usually, one of three circumstances must come into play in order for the IAEA to determine that it should request a special inspection and concentrate that inspection on a specific site or area:

1. A substantial accident or leakage occurs in the operation of a site that exposes the undeclared activities and is of such a magnitude as to be detected.
2. Intelligence information is supplied to the IAEA by a member state.
3. A random discovery is made during a routine inspection.

Otherwise, existing techniques, including wide-area environmental sampling, have limited detection ability. As an illustration, consider that Iran is 1.648 million km^2 in area, but wide-area environmental sampling is effective only within a range of 50 km. The effectiveness of this technique can be further reduced by bad weather conditions, infrequency of sample collection, and so forth.

The problem of limited technological capabilities is also illustrated by the following example: an accidental release of undeclared activity from ten to twenty centrifuges can be detected (1) only up to 10 km from its origin, and (2) only if there is prior data on the background radiation in the area that can be compared with the new data. Other technical tools (e.g., satellite imagery) will have similar limited detection capability if the IAEA does not have prior knowledge of the specific locations at which undeclared activities are taking place.[76]

Other means that a state can employ to prevent the IAEA from detecting its undeclared activities include building undeclared sites either underground or within or near a restricted area (e.g., a military base or religious site), and concentrating uranium activities in areas where the background radiation is already high.[77] Building undeclared facilities underground would be relatively easy for Iran, which, in addition to mining, has maintained a sophisticated network of tunnels over the centuries to carry irrigation water from the mountains down to the fields in the eastern part of the country.[78]

The preceding analysis raises serious questions about the IAEA's ability to detect nuclear activity in undeclared sites without prior information—especially national technical means supplied by an IAEA member state—that enables it to concentrate its safeguards efforts on a specific area, if not a specific site. It is essential that the IAEA possess this prior knowledge.

NOTES

1. See appendix 1 for a list (with accompanying map) of Iranian nuclear facilities under IAEA safeguards.
2. "IAEA Visit to Iran," IAEA press release, PR 1992/11, February 14, 1992.
3. David Kyd (IAEA spokesman), personal correspondence with the author, July 30, 2001.
4. Ibid. In addition, inspectors did not visit some of the scheduled sites because of bad weather. See also Kenneth Katzman, *Iran: U.S. Policy and Options,* Congressional Research Service Report for Congress (Washington, D.C.: Congressional Research Service, Library of Congress, January 14, 2000). Also available online

(www.globalsecurity.org/military/library/report/crs/97-231_000114.pdf).

5. Mark D. Skootsky, "U.S. Nuclear Policy toward Iran," *Nonproliferation Analysis* 1, no. 1 (June 1, 1995). Available online (http://infomanage.com/nonproliferation/najournal/iranuspolicy.html).

6. "IAEA Visit to Iran."

7. Rodney W. Jones et al., *Tracking Nuclear Proliferation: A Guide in Maps and Charts, 1998* (Washington, D.C.: Carnegie Endowment for International Peace, 1998), p. 171. Also available online (www.ceip.org/programs/npp/track98b.htm).

8. Skootsky, "U.S. Nuclear Policy toward Iran."

9. Mark Hibbs, "IAEA Says It Found No Non-Peaceful Activity During Recent Iran Visit," *Nucleonics Week* 34, no. 50 (December 16, 1993), p. 10.

10. Jones et al., *Tracking Nuclear Proliferation,* p. 171.

11. Eric Arnett, *Iran, Threat Perception and Military Confidence-Building Measures* (Stockholm International Peace Research Institute, n.d.). Available online (http://projects.sipri.se/technology/Iran_CBM.html).

12. Ibid.

13. Ibid.

14. Ibid.

15. Mark Hibbs, "No Sign of Undeclared Activity at New Iranian Sites, IAEA Says," *Nucleonics Week* 38, no. 32 (August 7, 1997), p. 9.

16. *IRAN Weekly Press Digest* 13, no. 21 (May 22–26, 2000).

17. See *The Safeguards Implementation Report for 2001* (IAEA document GOV/2002/20), April 30, 2002, pp. 12–13.

18. Wilhelm Gmelin, "Implications for Nuclear Safeguards in the EU Countries," in *Tightening the Reins,* ed. Erwin Hackel and Gotthard Stein (Berlin: Springer, 2000), p. 107.

19. *Strengthening the Effectiveness and Improving the Efficiency of the Safeguards System—Proposals for a Strengthened and More Efficient*

Safeguards System: A Report by the Director General (IAEA document GOV/2807), May 12, 1995, pp. 8–11, Articles 9–18.

20. Hans Hermann Remagen and Bernd Richter, "Implications for Research and Development in Safeguards Technology," in *Tightening the Reins,* ed. Erwin Hackel and Gotthard Stein (Berlin: Springer, 2000), p. 123.

21. Bruno Pellaud and Richard Hooper, "IAEA Safeguards in the 1990s: Building from Experience," *IAEA Bulletin* 37, no. 1 (March 1997). Also available online (www.iaea.org/worldatom/Periodicals/Bulletin/Bull371/pellaud.html).

22. *Strengthening the Effectiveness,* pp. 12–14, Articles 23–28.

23. Pellaud and Hooper, "IAEA Safeguards in the 1990s."

24. *The Structure and Content of Agreements between the Agency and States Required in Connection with the Treaty on the Non-Proliferation of Nuclear Weapons* (IAEA document INFCIRC/153 [Corrected], June 1972), article 116. Available online (www.iaea.org/worldatom/Documents/Infcircs/Others/inf153.shtml).

25. See Iran's General Debate statement at the 44th IAEA General Conference (Vienna, Austria, September 18, 2000); available online (www.iaea.org/worldatom/About/GC/GC44/Statements). A relevant quote by another senior Iranian diplomat can be found in Mark Hibbs, "Iran Won't Accept More Inspections unless U.S. Stops Nuclear Blockade," *Nucleonics Week* (June 1, 2000), p. 14.

26. *Statement by H.E. Mr. Hadi Nejad-Hosseinian, Ambassador and Permanent Representative of the Islamic Republic of Iran to the United Nations, on Agenda Item 14: Report of the International Atomic Energy Agency* (New York: November 2, 1998). Available online (www.un.int/iran/statements/generalassembly/session53/6.html).

27. "The United States shall apply, and permit the Agency to apply, this Protocol excluding only instances where its application would result in access by the Agency to activities with direct national security significance to the United States or to locations or information associated with such activities." *Protocol Additional to the Agreement between the United States of America and the International Atomic Energy Agency for the Application of Safeguards in the United*

States of America (IAEA document GOV/1998/24), May 14, 1998, Article I (b), (c).

28. Statement made by Mohamed Sadegh Ayatollahi, Iran's permanent representative to the IAEA, at the 913th Meeting of the IAEA board of governors, May 15, 1997, Vienna, Austria. See *Record of the Nine Hundred and Thirteenth Meeting* (IAEA document GOV/OR.913), p. 21; available online (www.iaea.org/worldatom/About/GC/GC41/documents/govor913.pdf).

29. Arnett, *Iran, Threat Perception.*

30. Statement by Mohamed Sadegh Ayatollahi, p. 21.

31. Elaine L. Morton et al., *Thinking Beyond the Stalemate in U.S.-Iranian Relations, Vol. I: Policy Review* (Washington, D.C.: Atlantic Council of the United States, May 2001), p. 22. Also available online (www.acus.org/publications).

32. Statement by Mohamed Sadegh Ayatollahi, p. 21.

33. Federation of American Scientists, "Iranian Revolutionary Guard Corps (IRGC)," in *Iran Special Weapons Guide,* n.d. Available online (www.fas.org/nuke/guide/iran/agency/irgc.htm).

34. See Farideh Farhi, "To Have or Not To Have? Iran's Domestic Debate on Nuclear Options," in *Iran's Nuclear Weapons Options: Issues and Analysis,* ed. Geoffrey Kemp (Washington, D.C.: Nixon Center, 2001), pp. 35–54, also available online (www.nixoncenter.org); and Mark Hibbs, "Khatami Not in Control of Iran's Nuclear Program, U.S. Believes," *Nucleonics Week* 39, no. 3 (January 15, 1998), p. 11.

35. Wolfgang Fischer, "Nuclear Nonproliferation and Safeguards: From INFCIRC/153 to INFCIRC/540 and Beyond," in *Tightening the Reins,* ed. Erwin Hackel and Gotthard Stein (Berlin: Springer, 2000), pp. 17–19.

36. A "significant quantity" has been defined by the IAEA as the amount of material that a country would need to make its first nuclear explosive device (i.e., 8 kg of plutonium or 25 kg of uranium enriched to 20 percent or more in uranium-235, or 8 kg of uranium-233.)

37. Shaun Burnie, "The IAEA and the NPT Safeguards Regime: An Impossible Task," in *Beyond the Bomb: The Extension of the Nonpro-*

liferation Treaty and the Future of Nuclear Weapons (based on a series of five international seminars held at the Transnational Institute in Amsterdam, Netherlands, Spring 1995), ed. Huub Jaspers (Amsterdam: Transnational Institute, July 1996). Also available online (www.antenna.nl/wise/beyondbomb/2-2.html).

38. "Treaty on the Non-Proliferation of Nuclear Weapons," no. 10485 in *United Nations Treaty Series,* vol. 729 (New York: United Nations, 1968), pp. 169–75, Article X. The text of the treaty is also available online (www.unog.ch/disarm/distreat/npt.pdf).

39. Kenneth R. Timmerman, "Iran's Nuclear Program: Myth and Reality," in *Fifty Years of Nuclear Weapons: Proceedings of the Sixth Castiglioncello Conference* (Milan: Italian Union of Scientists for Disarmament [USPID], 1996). Also available online (www.uspid.dsi.unimi.it/proceed/cast95/index.html).

40. Anthony H. Cordesman, *Proliferation in the 'Axis of Evil': North Korea, Iran, and Iraq* (Washington, D.C.: Center for Strategic and International Studies, January 30, 2002), p. 23 (statement made in an October 1988 Iranian parliamentary debate).

41. Jonathan B. Tucker, "Monitoring and Verification in a Noncooperative Environment: Lessons from the U.N. Experience in Iraq," *Nonproliferation Review* 3, no. 3 (Spring–Summer 1996), p. 9. Also available online (http://cns.miis.edu/pubs/npr/vol03/33/tucker33.pdf).

42. Abram N. Shulsky, "Elements of Strategic Denial and Deception," in *Strategic Denial and Deception: The Twenty-First Century Challenge,* ed. Roy Godson and James J. Wirtz (Piscataway, N.J.: Transaction, 2002).

43. David Kay, "Iraqi Inspections: Lessons Learned," in *Iraq Special Collection,* n.d., Center for Nonproliferation Studies. Adapted from the transcript of a talk given for the Program of Nonproliferation Studies, Monterey Institute of International Studies, February 10, 1993. Available online (www.cns.miis.edu/research/iraq/kay.htm).

44. David Kay, "Denial and Deception: The Lessons of Iraq," in *U.S. Intelligence at the Crossroads,* ed. Roy Godson, Ernest R. May, and Gary Schmitt (Washington, D.C.: Brassey's, 1995), p. 111.

45. Iran has admitted that it had a chemical weapons program at the end of the Iraq-Iran War but claims that it currently possesses no

chemical weapons and that all of the facilities developed during the war have been destroyed.

46. Federation of American Scientists, "Chemical Weapons," in *Iran Special Weapons Guide,* n.d. Available online (www.fas.org/nuke/guide/iran/cw/index.html).

47. *Statement by H.E. Ambassador Mohammad R. Alborzi, Director General of the Ministry of Foreign Affairs, Head of Delegation of the Islamic Republic of Iran to the Third Session of the Conference of the States Parties of the Chemical Weapons Convention, The Hague, the Netherlands,* 53rd session, November 19, 1998. Available online (www.un.int/iran/statements/firstcommittee/session53/5.html).

48. Office of the Director of Central Intelligence, *Unclassified Report to Congress on the Acquisition of Technology Relating to Weapons of Mass Destruction and Advanced Conventional Munitions, 1 January through 30 June 2001.* Available online (www.cia.gov/cia/publications/bian/bian_jan_2002.htm#3).

49. See *Worldwide Threat: Converging Dangers in a Post 9/11 World: Testimony of Director of Central Intelligence George J. Tenet before the Senate Select Committee on Intelligence,* February 6, 2002; available online (www.cia.gov/cia/public_affairs/speeches/dci_speech_ 02062002.html). See also John Diamond, "Israel: Iran Could Have Nuclear Arms in 5 Years," *Chicago Tribune,* February 8, 2002.

50. David Albright and Corey Hinderstein, "Algeria: Big Deal in the Desert?" *Bulletin of the Atomic Scientists* 57, no. 3 (May–June 2001), pp. 45–52. Also available online (www.thebulletin.org/issues/2001/mj01/mj01albright.html).

51. Ibid.

52. Statement by the president of the Security Council at the UNSC meeting of heads of state, S/23500, January 31, 1992. Available online (http://projects.sipri.se/cbw/docs/cbw-unsc23500.html).

53. *Vienna Convention on the Law of Treaties,* May 23, 1969, UN Doc A/Conf 39/28, UKTS 58 (1980), 8 ILM 679, Article 18.

54. Mark W. Janis, *An Introduction to International Law,* 3rd ed. (Gaithersburg, Md.: Aspen Law & Business, 1999), p. 21.

55. Ibid.

56. *Model Protocol Additional to the Agreement(s) between State(s) and the International Atomic Energy Agency for the Application of Safeguards* (IAEA document INFCIRC/540), September 1997, pp. 13–14, Article 17. Available online (www.iaea.org/worldatom/Documents/Infcircs/1997/infcirc540.pdf).

57. For examples of Russian policy statements regarding Russian cooperation with Iran, see two statements delivered at the 2001 Carnegie International Nonproliferation Conference: Marshal Igor Sergeyev, advisor on strategic stability to President Vladimir Putin, English translation of untitled speech, June 18, 2001, available online (www.ceip.org/files/projects/npp/resources/Conference%202001/sergeyev.htm); and Vladimir Rybachenkov, Russian Ministry of Foreign Affairs, "Dealing with Iran" panel, June 19, 2001, available online (www.ceip.org/files/projects/npp/resources/Conference%202001/Panels/iran.htm).

58. Statement by Mohamed Sadegh Ayatollahi, p. 22.

59. Tucker, "Monitoring and Verification," p. 4.

60. Ibid., p. 7.

61. Ibid., p. 9.

62. Ibid.

63. Kay, "Iraqi Inspections: Lessons Learned."

64. Ibid.

65. Daniel Horner, "IAEA Added Protocol May Help U.S., Russia End Impasse over Russian Aid to Iran," *Nuclear Fuel* 27, no. 12 (June 10, 2002), p. 15 (paraphrasing of statements by Robert Einhorn, former U.S. assistant secretary of state for nonproliferation).

66. Tucker, "Monitoring and Verification," p. 9.

67. Kay, "Denial and Deception: The Lessons of Iraq," pp. 113–15.

68. The NSG is an export control arrangement that contributes to the nonproliferation of nuclear weapons by implementing guidelines for the control of nuclear and nuclear-related exports. Members pursue the aims of the NSG through voluntary adherence to the guidelines (which are adopted by consensus) and through the exchange of information.

69. Tucker, "Monitoring and Verification," p. 1.

70. Ibid., p. 9. Iraq used electromagnetic isotope separation to produce highly enriched uranium.

71. Ibid.

72. Kay, "Denial and Deception: The Lessons of Iraq," p. 119. Similarly, before UN inspections of sensitive sites, the Iraqis often "found excuses ranging from transportation bottlenecks to bad weather to delay the U.N. team's arrival and buy time to remove incriminating evidence." Tucker, "Monitoring and Verification," p. 8.

73. Dimitri Perricos, "Uncovering the Secret Program: Initial Inspections" (paper presented at the conference "Understanding the Lessons of Nuclear Inspections and Monitoring in Iraq: A Ten-Year Review," sponsored by the Institute for Science and International Security, Washington, D.C., June 14–15, 2001). Available online (www.isis-online.org/publications/iraq/perricos.html).

74. Kay, "Denial and Deception: The Lessons of Iraq," p. 120.

75. Fischer, "Nuclear Nonproliferation and Safeguards," p. 16.

76. Jacques Baute (team leader of the IAEA Action Team), "Nuclear Disarmament and Ongoing Monitoring and Verification in Iraq" (presentation at the IAEA Symposium on International Safeguards entitled "Verification and Nuclear Material Security," Vienna, Austria, October 29–November 2, 2001).

77. Many such areas exist in Iran; moreover, in some Iranian cities natural radiation is higher than the recommended level.

78. Helen Chapin Metz, ed., *Iran: A Country Study*, rev. ed. (Washington, D.C.: Library of Congress, Federal Research Division, December 1987). Also available online (http://lcweb2.loc.gov/frd/cs/irtoc.html).

Chapter 4

Program 93+2 in Regional Context

The new IAEA verification system goes a long way toward strengthening the agency's ability to detect undeclared activities. Even after Program 93+2 is widely adopted, however, problems will remain—some are rooted in the NPT verification system itself; others are technical, political, or organizational in nature.

The advantages and disadvantages of the current IAEA safeguards system can be compared to those in a different kind of verification regime: a regional organization responsible for verifying the nonproliferation of nuclear weapons (and preferably all WMD) in the Middle East. Examples of similar organizations include: OPANAL, the Agency for the Prohibition of Nuclear Weapons in Latin America and the Caribbean[1]; ABACC, the Brazilian-Argentine Agency for Accounting and Control of Nuclear Materials; and EURATOM, the European Atomic Energy Community.

The notion of establishing a regional nonproliferation agreement in the Middle East has been discussed for nearly three decades. In 1974, after the Yom Kippur War—realizing the potential for nuclear war to break out in the Middle East through a clash between the two superpowers, and heeding the growing speculation that Israel was developing nuclear weapons capabilities—Iran and Egypt proposed a resolution in the UN General Assembly establishing a "nuclear weapons–free zone" (NWFZ) in the

Middle East. In 1981, a revised resolution passed in the General Assembly and has been readopted every year by a consensus vote of UN member states, including all Middle Eastern states.

On April 18, 1990, President Hosni Mubarak of Egypt launched an initiative for expanding the idea of a NWFZ in the Middle East into a "weapons of mass destruction–free zone" (WMDFZ). This initiative called for the prohibition of all forms of weapons of mass destruction, urged all Middle Eastern countries to exchange equal commitments toward that end, and called for the development of an accurate system of examining the implementation of these commitments.[2] This initiative has been the basis of several "track-two" diplomacy forums (as well as Arab League efforts) aimed at drafting an agreement on a WMDFZ in the region.

In 1991, Israel and the Arab states held unprecedented direct discussions on arms control issues in general and on establishing a WMDFZ in the Middle East in particular. These discussions took place under the auspices of the Arms Control and Regional Security (ACRS) working group,

> one of five multilateral groups formed shortly after the opening round of the Middle East Peace Process in Madrid in October 1991. . . . Thirteen Arab states, Israel, a Palestinian delegation, and over a score of extra-regional entities participate[d] in plenary and intercessional meetings focusing on both conceptual and operational confidence building and arms control measures applicable to the Middle East.[3]

In addition, some ACRS meetings took the form of special site visits:

> Parties toured a German nuclear power plant and discussed the interaction between the IAEA and its

> regional verification authority, EURATOM. Parties toured a Swiss chemical weapon verification laboratory and a Finnish chemical weapon verification–related training facility as a part of a workshop on implementation of the Chemical Weapons Convention.[4]

At the end of 1995, however, the talks were put on hold indefinitely, partly due to complications in the peace process, but also due to increasing disagreement between Israel and Egypt on the question of when to place discussion of an NWFZ on the ACRS agenda.[5]

Specifically, Egypt argued that the nuclear issue should be addressed immediately and called for Israel to sign the NPT. Israel's position, however, has been that all regional security issues—including the nuclear issue—should be handled within the context of a successful regional peace process. Israel supports the eventual establishment of a mutually verifiable NWFZ in the Middle East. Yet, it also believes that the political realities of the region mandate a step-by-step approach. This approach would begin with modest confidence-building measures aimed at creating a stable environment of peace and reconciliation, followed by the establishment of peaceful relations and, perhaps, complemented by various arms control measures.[6]

From the Israeli perspective, neither a WMDFZ nor an NWFZ can be established in a region where states declare themselves to be at war with Israel, refuse in principle to maintain peaceful relations with Israel, or deny Israel's right to exist.[7] Still, discussions continue on an informal basis despite these disagreements, and many regional parties attend numerous track-two events per year.

VERIFICATION CONSTRAINTS

Certain limitations are inherent in any verification process—for example, the NPT as a multilateral treaty can achieve only so much by means of its political, technical, and legal tools. Indeed, the current IAEA safeguards regime cannot by itself prevent a violation:

> The system is designed as an early warning mechanism to initiate the necessary procedures for remedial action in case of violation. Under the IAEA Statute, non-compliance with safeguards obligations is to be reported to the United Nations Security Council for appropriate action. . . . [S]afeguards cannot assess the future intentions of states. The system can be analogized to a radar device which can only report on the existing situation.[8]

In other words, the verification system can only provide notification if discrepancies are found.

An additional limitation of IAEA safeguards is the difficulty of finding a state in noncompliance since inspections rarely turn up clear-cut evidence of a violation. Indeed, the accomplishments of the IAEA were limited even under the most intrusive verification regime—that which was applied in Iraq as part of UNSC Resolution 687. This resolution conferred on inspectors wide-ranging and unprecedented powers, none of which are granted by the INFCIRC/153 or Additional Protocol safeguards agreements.[9] Nevertheless, ever since the seizure of "smoking gun documents" during the 1991 "parking lot" incident,[10] most of the important new information about Iraqi WMD development has been provided by Iraqi defectors, not by verification mechanisms.

The current objectives of the IAEA, as an international system, are to detect and deter, but a regional system must also be able to warn. At the regional level, the threat of a breach is tangible to each state's immediate security, and in a region that suffers from bitter mistrust, even the strictest measures cannot produce confidence of the kind necessary for neighboring states to feel secure; these measures are effective only when states demonstrate political will on a long-term basis. A system that is unable to warn of an impending violation cannot guarantee states that they will enhance their own security by joining the regime.

A regional framework can also treat special inspections differently. Under the IAEA verification regime, a special inspection is considered a rare event, and one that sharply increases political tension. A request for a special inspection in locations identified according to the expanded declaration as "having no nuclear material" must be submitted with "specific reasons" before inspectors are granted access by the state. Delays and disagreements as to whether the IAEA has good reason to conduct such an inspection are bound to ensue.

In a regional regime, a request for a special inspection is viewed less as a political tool and more as a clarifying mechanism. Under several existing regional verification regimes, it is the regional agency—in the event that lower-level investigations are unsuccessful—that is responsible for requesting a special inspection in order to investigate complaints. For example, under the agreement for the Conventional Forces in Europe, no explanation need accompany a special inspection request. Here, a special inspection can serve as a "fact-finding mission" to clarify and resolve situations that may be considered ambiguous or that may give rise to doubts about a state's compliance with the provisions of the treaty.[11]

Two other verification measures that can be used freely by a regional regime are random and no- or short-notice inspections aimed at reducing the window of opportunity within which a state can carry out undeclared activities. The IAEA has never used such inspections.

Organizational Constraints

Other problems specific to the IAEA verification regime are rooted in the agency's organizational structure and objectives.

Conflicting Objectives. One of the IAEA's primary mandates, according to its statute, is to promote the peaceful uses of nuclear energy. But while the IAEA is sponsoring extensive technical assistance programs in states such as Iraq, Iran, North Korea, Algeria, and Libya, the agency is also mandated to ensure that these civil programs are not used for military purposes. Moreover, many developing countries (especially India and Iran) believe that promoting the transfer of nuclear technology should be the IAEA's top priority.

The tension between these two mandates is primarily a result of the agency's budgetary constraints. The IAEA has been operating under a budget with zero real growth over the last fifteen years, while the safeguards activities it is required to perform are growing extensively. The overall agency budget is currently about $230 million.

In contrast to the IAEA and its clashing objectives (at least from a budgetary standpoint), a regional verification organization in the Middle East must have one clear objective: to ensure the absence of nuclear weapons and undeclared nuclear activities in the region. Promoting the peaceful uses of nuclear energy should not be the primary objective of such a regime.

Political Considerations. Other organizational problems specific to the IAEA derive from the international nature of the agency. In international regimes, issues such as defining what constitutes "cheating," determining who is threatened by such deception, and deciding how seriously violators should be treated have become complicated political decisions. Noncompliance by certain states may pose little or no security threat to other states party to the treaty. Accordingly, Middle Eastern parties to the NPT have shown little interest in decrying North Korean noncompliance, just as East Asian states have shown little interest in the Iraqi problem. Cheating that does not put states at material risk is unlikely to result in an act of political enforcement.[12]

In a regional verification system, however, a violation by a state would not be met with indifference. The threat that a violation poses to regional stability—or even the less immediate danger of a proliferation chain effect—would impel member states to take immediate action minimizing the threat.

Nondiscrimination. Because the IAEA is required to function under the norms of an international organization, it is also obliged to adhere to the nondiscrimination rule, which poses another structural problem. In the context of the application of safeguards, the nondiscrimination rule means that the number, intensity, duration, timing, and mode of routine IAEA inspections performed under INFCIRC/153 are determined by quantitative criteria such as the amount and form of nuclear material a state possesses, the effectiveness of a state's accounting and control systems, and the characteristics of a state's nuclear fuel cycle. Thus, when the IAEA decides on how many inspections to conduct or what measures to apply, it does not take into account factors such as the risk of proliferation or diversion because these are not quantifiable criteria. This problem resulted in an absurd situation at the time of the Gulf War, during which more than 80 percent of the IAEA's inspections budget was allocated to carrying out inspections in states whose highly developed nuclear energy programs did not raise proliferation concerns (e.g., Canada, Japan, and members of the European Community).

The Additional Protocol does attempt to address this problem, in that the expanded declaration that each member state is required to submit "would not be verified systematically or mechanistically." The meaning of this provision awaits clarification by IAEA practice, but apparently the agency would, under this protocol, be able to enforce safeguards less on the basis of correct qualitative accounting (especially in states not considered to be a proliferation risk) than on the basis of a country's nonproliferation credentials.

Political pressure to observe the nondiscrimination criteria, however, may force the IAEA to take the path of narrow legal interpretation, using its right of complementary access to verify the expanded declaration only when inconsistencies arise. With this approach, the IAEA is often accused of maintaining a "don't rock the boat" policy; that is, inspections seek to confirm compliance, not to discern noncompliance, while inspectors are not encouraged to question activities or facilities outside of defined strategic points. According to several pre–Gulf War inspectors in Iraq, asking too many questions often led to difficulties with both Iraqi officials and IAEA headquarters[13]; some would say that this problem persists today.

Nondiscrimination limitations on the IAEA also constrain the agency in its selection of inspectors because it must take into account national and geographical distribution. Moreover, the IAEA is limited by previously mentioned budgetary problems.

Under a regional verification system, mutual inspections serve to counter this problem. A mutual inspection is more effective than an international inspection for at least three reasons.[14] First, in the regional model, states have the freedom to choose the best professionals from relevant fields without the same constraints as an international organization (e.g., budgetary limitations, nondiscrimination rules). Second, in the regional model, inspectors are more highly motivated to search for violations. Intrinsically, mutual inspections tend to foster an atmosphere in which investigations are carried out in a technically sound manner, not merely "by the book." In principle, because inspectors' motivations are free from conflicting interests, neither their sponsoring states nor the regional organization itself suffer political embarrassment in searching for or discovering violations.

Third, under a mutual verification system, inspectors have access to a broad base of information and support. Within such a system, inspectors go into the field with the full institutional backing of their country (and their country's intelligence services).

Political Constraints

Lack of political support is another limitation of the IAEA. The agency is not the secretariat of the NPT, nor is it empowered to enforce NPT compliance. Rather, in order to commence a special inspection that is refused by a state, the IAEA needs the backing of the UNSC, a political body whose five permanent members often act according to conflicting interests and internal power struggles. In effect, the UNSC is virtually useless in the face of noncompliance if there is no agreement among, and support from, all five permanent members. The result of such impotence is visible in the current UNSC deadlock over Iraq, or in the past impasse over North Korea.

The decisionmaking process within a regional organization is different. In this kind of regime, decisions are made by state members directly responsible for ensuring the application of the original agreement, which in turn is aimed at strengthening the security and stability of the region. Although a regional mechanism represents participants' individual interests, it is also responsible for dealing with the localized consequences of noncompliance. Decisions are not made by a political body removed from the region, with political or economic interests that are sometimes irrelevant to nonproliferation.

Technical Constraints

The IAEA is also limited by technical constraints, some of which have been mentioned. Expert analysis by the U.S. Department of Energy[15] confirmed recently that the 8-kg plutonium threshold set in the 1960s is now too high and should be lowered,[16] as the new, more advanced methods of assembling a nuclear explosive device require only 4 kg of plutonium.[17] Lower thresholds, however, would have required a tremendous increase in the number of inspections, so many that the IAEA might have found it difficult to carry them out.[18]

Moreover, since the IAEA lacks direct expertise on nuclear weapons,

> it relies on the nuclear-weapon states for technical advice on matters such as the appropriate definition of [a significant quantity]. Existing definitions date back to . . . the mid-1960s; in the absence of subsequent guidance, the IAEA had no basis to revise them. . . . In 1990, [IAEA] Director General Blix asked the nuclear-weapon states to provide updated guidance on whether the definitions should be revised. He received no response.[19]

States putting their security in the hands of an international regime such as the IAEA find it difficult to tolerate the agency's limited ability to adapt to changing realities.

A similar problem with technical adaptation lies in the area of timely detection. The IAEA defines timely detection as "the estimated time that would be needed to convert diverted material into components of a nuclear explosive device." The timeframes vary "according to the nature of the material: . . . 7–10 days for plutonium or high-enriched uranium in metallic form (the so-called 'direct-use' material); 1–3 months for plutonium in spent reactor fuel; and about one year for natural or low-enriched uranium."[20] But if "timely" as understood in the U.S. Nuclear Nonproliferation Act (1978) should also allow for "diplomatic action to prevent the fabrication and insertion of the diverted material into a first bomb," then the threshold for detection time should be "even shorter than conversion time, in order to allow for evaluation and response."[21] Here, however, as in the case of "significant quantity," the IAEA has received no new formal technical guidance from member states and therefore has not yet updated the frequency of its inspections.

Participation Constraints

Other IAEA limitations are rooted in Program 93+2 itself. One such obstacle is limited participation. As mentioned previously, there is no timeframe within which an INFCIRC/153 state must adopt the Additional Protocol, and the IAEA is not currently active in persuading states to adopt it. As of May 2002, 61 of the 187 NPT states had signed the protocol, and only 25 had taken the steps necessary for it to enter into force (see appendix 3).

The membership of states whose participation is deemed important is one fundamental of a nonproliferation regime's effectiveness. Overall participation in the Additional Protocol is currently at 30 percent, and only one Middle Eastern state has adopted the protocol. Such participation levels are not sufficient to either strengthen the acceptance of nonproliferation as a norm or reassure those states that hoped to enhance their security by joining the regime.

Regional arrangements are even more dependent on the participation of key states. Unlike the Additional Protocol—in which individual states are responsible only for the entry into force of their own agreement with the IAEA—regional NWFZ agreements do not effectively enter into force until those states with the most advanced nuclear programs become full members. This was true in the case of the Treaty of Tlatelolco, which Argentina and Brazil fully adopted only twenty-five years after it was opened for signature. Negotiations pertaining to the Pelindaba Treaty (the African Nuclear Weapon–Free Zone

Treaty) began in 1962 but did not conclude until 1996, following South Africa's decision to dismantle its nuclear weapons and join the NPT as a NNWS in 1995.

The Middle East is even more problematic in this sense because some states in the region (including Iran) do not recognize Israel's right to exist and thus refuse even to sit at the same negotiating table with Israeli counterparts.[22] These kinds of participation constraints make a regional agreement seem unrealistic in the current political reality.

NOTES

1. Established under the 1967 Treaty for the Prohibition of Nuclear Weapons in Latin America and the Caribbean (Treaty of Tlatelolco).
2. The "Mubarak Initiative" (letter from the deputy prime minister and minister of foreign affairs of Egypt to the UN secretary general, April 16, 1990).
3. Bureau of Public Affairs, U.S. Department of State, *Middle East Peace Process Arms Control and Regional Security (ACRS) Working Group,* fact sheet (Washington, D.C., July 1, 2001). Available online (www.state.gov/t/pm/rls/fs/2001/4271.htm).
4. Ibid.
5. Emily Landau, *Egypt and Israel in ACRS: Bilateral Concerns in a Regional Arms Control Process,* Memorandum no. 59 (Tel Aviv: Jaffee Center for Strategic Studies, Tel Aviv University, June 2001), p. 18. Also available online (www.tau.ac.il/jcss/memoranda/memo59.pdf).
6. "The Establishment of a Nuclear Weapons–Free Zone in the Middle East," statement made by Israeli representatives on the First Committee (Disarmament and International Security) at the 56th Session of the United Nations General Assembly, November 29, 2001. Available online (www.israel-un.org/committees/first/Theestab.htm).

7. Ibid.

8. Mohamed ElBaradei, Edwin Nwogugu, and John Rames, "International Law and Nuclear Energy: Overview of the Legal Framework," *IAEA Bulletin* 37, no. 3 (September 1995). Also available online (www.iaea.org/worldatom/Periodicals/Bulletin/Bull373/bulletinv37n3.html).

9. Gideon Frank, concluding remarks at the Institute for Science and International Security seminar "Argentina and Brazil: The Latin American Nuclear Rapprochement," Nahel Soreq, Israel, May 16, 1996. Available online (www.isis-online.org/publications/israel96/596pm2.html).

10. The IAEA's sixth onsite inspection team (September 20–21, 1991) was detained for four days in a Baghdad parking lot after seizing documents related to Iraq's nuclear weapons program. The documents were forcibly confiscated by Iraqi authorities; although most were returned to the inspectors a few hours later, Iraq did not return any documents referring to PC-3 Group Four (the research group responsible for Iraq's nuclear weaponization effort). See *IAEA Iraq Action Team: Chronology of Main Events,* May 21, 2002. Available online (www.iaea.org/worldatom/Programmes/ActionTeam/chronology.html).

11. Such terms can also be found in the December 15, 1995, "Treaty on the Southeast Asia Nuclear Weapon–Free Zone (Bangkok Treaty)," reprinted in *Inventory of International Nonproliferation Organizations and Regimes,* rev. ed. (Monterey, Calif.: Monterey Institute of International Studies, August 2000), pp. 160–68. Also available online (http://cns.miis.edu/pubs/inven/inven2k.pdf).

12. Brad Roberts, "Revisiting Fred Iklé's 1961 Question, 'After Detection—What?,'" *Nonproliferation Review* 8, no. 1 (Spring 2001), p. 14.

13. Lawrence Scheinman, *Assuring the Nuclear Nonproliferation Safeguards System* (Washington, D.C.: Atlantic Council of the United States, May 2001), p. 27. Quoted in David Kay, "Iraq and Beyond: Future Nonproliferation Inspection Challenges" (Nonproliferation Policy Education Center, March 1996); available online (www.npec-web.org/pages/papers.htm).

14. Frank, "Argentina and Brazil."

15. Kathleen Hart, "NRDC Seeks Drastic Reduction in IAEA Nuclear Threshold Figure," *Nucleonics Week* 35, no. 34 (August 28, 1994), p. 12 (quoting Thomas Cochran, a senior scientist at the Natural Resources Defense Council).

16. Jozef Goldblat, "Implementation of Article III of the NPT" (paper presented at the seminar "Nonproliferation: Point of View from Latin America and the Caribbean," Cancun, Mexico, January 11–15, 1995). Available online (www.opanal.org/Articles/cancun/can-Goldblat.htm).

17. Office of Technology Assessment, U.S. Congress, *Nuclear Safeguards and the International Atomic Energy Agency,* OTA-ISS-615 (Washington, D.C.: U.S. Government Printing Office, 1995), p. 67. Also available online (www.wws.princeton.edu/~ota/disk1/1995/9530.html).

18. "In 1979, the IAEA was only able to completely attain 27 percent of the inspection goals it set for itself, although for material directly usable in weapons its goal attainment was 60 percent. By 1984, this record had improved to 53 percent for all materials and 71 percent for weapon-usable materials. At major facilities, the IAEA attained 63 percent of its inspection goals in 1986 and 81 percent in 1990 before dropping back to 69 percent in 1992." Ibid., p. 49. According to its most recent Safeguards Implementation Report, the IAEA attained around 85 percent of its inspection goals. See *The Safeguards Implementation Report for 2001* (IAEA document GOV/2002/20), April 30, 2002, para. 96.

19. Office of Technology Assessment, *Nuclear Safeguards,* p. 68.

20. Goldblat, "Implementation of Article III of the NPT."

21. Marvin M. Miller, *Are IAEA Safeguards on Plutonium Bulk-Handling Facilities Effective?* (Washington, D.C.: Nuclear Control Institute, August 1990). Available online (www.nci.org/k-m/mmsgrds.htm).

22. Iran, Iraq, Syria, Lebanon, and Libya did not participate in the ACRS group that met as part of the multilateral talks (1992–1995).

Conclusion

You change for only two reasons: you learn enough that you want to, or you hurt enough that you have to.

—Randall D. Worley

Program 93+2 represents an important step in strengthening efforts to prevent the proliferation of nuclear weapons. In the 1990s, the international community faced a severe crisis with the discovery that the existing IAEA safeguards system failed to detect the clandestine Iraqi and North Korean nuclear programs. The Program 93+2 initiative to strengthen IAEA detection capabilities by expanding the agency's mandate was birthed from this crisis, and from the recognition that these two states, although parties to the NPT and certified to be in full compliance with the treaty's safeguards obligations, had successfully developed clandestine nuclear weapons programs by using an impressive variety of deception and denial techniques.

Program 93+2 can and should bring about a more reliable verification regime toward precluding a recurrence of the Iraq and North Korea experiences. In this regard, the program brings some important new powers to the IAEA in terms of detecting undeclared activities. Part I of Program 93+2 provides measures that, although extant under the IAEA's old mandate, had not previously been implemented; these measures are aimed at exposing undeclared activities in declared sites as well as preventing diversion of declared materials from those sites. Part II (the Additional Protocol) provides the IAEA with measures facilitating the exposure of undeclared activities in undeclared sites, a right that the agency did not previously possess.

Yet, Program 93+2 addresses only two of the paths, parallel program and diversion, available to a state pursuing nuclear weapons development. The other available paths, especially an open violation of or withdrawal from the NPT, remain unaddressed by the Additional Protocol. Although the existence of unaddressed paths is a serious concern, the related problems (and their solutions) are concentrated at the political and legal—not the technical or safeguards—levels, and thus fall outside the IAEA mandate and the scope of this paper. The effectiveness of future IAEA safeguards with regard to the paths that the Additional Protocol does cover will depend to a great extent on both IAEA decisiveness and the political support that the agency receives from both IAEA member states and the UNSC. Under the old safeguards system, the IAEA conducted its verification missions according to nondiscrimination criteria, spending 80 percent of its efforts in states whose highly developed nuclear energy programs did not raise proliferation concerns (e.g., Canada, Japan, and members of the European Community).

But under the Additional Protocol, the IAEA can manage its verification efforts with less concern for nondiscrimination criteria, focusing more on a country's nonproliferation credentials. Such a proactive attitude would reduce the ability of a state to use deception or denial techniques without being detected. As of today, the IAEA has chosen to avoid conflict or situations that might cause embarrassment to inspected states. But the effectiveness of the new safeguards regime will rest on the agency's determination to adopt a "no trust" posture, conducting no-notice or special inspections even in INFCIRC/153 states.

Alternatively, the IAEA may choose to continue avoiding conflict by adopting a narrow legal interpretation of the protocol, using its right to complementary access only on an event-driven basis, after inconsistencies have arisen. The agency is effectively choosing a passive option when it waits for discrepancies to arise rather than searching for them, or when it concentrates on verifying a given declaration's correctness alone, ignoring its completeness.

Because Iran rejects any allegations that it is developing nuclear weapons, its policy toward the Additional Protocol can be viewed as a test case with regard to the country's NPT and other nonproliferation commitments. If Iran enters directly or indirectly into negotiations with the IAEA on the adoption of the Additional Protocol, any resulting agreement should include a timetable for both signature and ratification, since Iran will delay accession whether or not it chooses to develop nuclear weapons. If Tehran does not intend to develop a clandestine program, it will delay by making its signature conditional upon maximizing political gains, technical cooperation, and economic support.

Alternately, should Iran choose to embark on a nuclear weapons program, it will sign, but not ratify, the protocol only after it overcomes all technical obstacles to the production of a nuclear weapon, obtains all the necessary materials, and, more likely than not, enters the early stages of fissile material production. Although Iran would be considered a party in good faith to the Additional Protocol's obligations if it signed without ratifying, from a practical standpoint the IAEA would not have the right to employ the protocol's verification and enforcement measures. Until Iran does ratify, the country's de facto safeguards obligations will remain limited to INFCIRC/153 (the IAEA's model full-scope safeguards agreement). Since the Iranian government has not yet incorporated Part I measures from Program 93+2, Iran's safeguards status is currently identical to that of Iraq prior to the Gulf War.

Even in the unlikely event that Iran decides to ratify the Additional Protocol, it is highly improbable that the IAEA would be able to detect illicit activities in undeclared sites that do not intersect with Iran's safeguarded civil nuclear program if no specific information on the violation is provided by an IAEA member state. A declaration by Iran that obliges it to avoid the enrichment, reprocessing, production, or acquisition of fissile material would be desirable; but Iran's agreement to this kind of declaration would probably only be achieved in the context of a bilateral cooperation agreement with another state. Still, such a precaution would reduce, but not fully eliminate, the possibility of Iran misusing the verification regime.

A regional nonproliferation regime might be a better option for the Middle East than an international regime because it offers flexibility with regard to adopting measures more relevant to the region, such as mutual inspections and lower thresholds for the triggering of safeguards. Given the special circumstances of the Middle East—where a relatively small amount of nuclear material exists and where suspicions about noncompliance are high[1]—these kinds of measures would not only increase the regional regime's ability to prevent the diversion of material sufficient to develop a nuclear device, but also strengthen the confidence of member states in the regime's ability to detect violators.

Because today a regional approach in the Middle East seems more hypothetical than ever, the Additional Protocol remains the best available mechanism in the region for restricting a state's ability to develop nuclear weapons. Although no system is foolproof, a stronger IAEA verification regime can build barriers and raise the price that Iran or any other state must pay—in money, time, and manpower—in order to successfully develop a clandestine nuclear program.

Notes

1. As of this writing, IAEA safeguards apply to nineteen nuclear sites in the Middle East (including nuclear power and research reactors). See the table "Facilities under Agency Safeguards or Containing Safeguarded Material on 31 December 2000," an addendum to the IAEA's *Annual Report for 2000;* available online (www.iaea.org/worldatom/Documents/Anrep/Anrep2000/table18_ext.pdf).

Appendices

ARM.
AZERBAIJAN
TURKMENISTAN
Caspian Sea
Bonab
Tabriz
TUR.
Lake Urmia
Rasht
Ramsar
Qazvin
Tehran
Mashad
Qom
Dasht-e Kavir
AFGHANISTAN
Esfahan
Dasht-e Lut
Yazd
IRAQ
Ahwaz
Abadan
Kerman
Shiraz
Bushehr
KUWAIT
IRAN
PAKISTAN
Persian Gulf
N
SAUDI ARABIA
0
250
miles
BAHRAIN
QATAR
Oman
U.A.E.
Gulf of Oman
Arabian Sea
D. Swanson/Equator Graphics, Inc.

Appendix 1: Iran's Nuclear Facilities under IAEA Safeguards Agreements or Subject to IAEA Visits (see map, opposite page)

Location	Name	Type	Under safeguards (subsidiary arrangements in force)	Comments
Bonab	Bonab Atomic Energy Research Center	Research on nuclear technology for agricultural uses	-	Visited by IAEA director general Hans Blix in July 1997
Bushehr	Bushehr 1	Power reactor	Not yet	Included in the Feb. 1992 IAEA visit; since nuclear materials have not yet been introduced, IAEA safeguards are not applied
	Bushehr 2	Power reactor	Not yet	
Esfahan	MNSR	Research reactor	+	Subsidiary arrangements completed after 1994
	HWZPR	Research reactor	+	Subsidiary arrangements completed after 1994
	LWSCR	Research reactor	+	
	GSCR	Research reactor	-	
		Fuel-fabrication laboratory	-	Subsidiary arrangements not yet completed
Qazvin	Moallem Kalayeh	Training/recreation facility	-	Included once in the Feb. 1992 IAEA visit
Ramsar	Nuclear research center	Research on nuclear radioactivity	-	Visited by IAEA director general Hans Blix in July 1997
Tehran	TRR	Research reactor	+	
	Sharif University of Technology	Alleged uranium centrifuge facility	-	Included once in the Nov. 1993 IAEA visit
	University of Tehran	Uranium-ore concentration facility	-	Included once in the Feb. 1992 IAEA visit
Yazd		Uranium deposits	-	Included once in the Feb. 1992 IAEA visit

Appendix 2: Measures Adopted under Program 93+2

Category of Measure		**Measure**	**Measures to be implemented under existing legal authority (Part I)**	**Measures proposed for implementation under complementary legal authority (Part II)**
Broader Access to Information	Expanded Declaration	1. Information on the SSAC	INFCIRC/153 paras. 7, 31, 32, 81(b); GOV/2784 para. 34	
		2.a. Information on past nuclear activities (decommissioned nuclear facilities and existing historical records on production of nuclear material) relevant to assessing the state's declarations of present nuclear activities, including the completeness and correctness of its initial report	INFCIRC/153 paras. 3, 62; GOV/2784 para. 35	
		2.b. Information presently routinely provided: (i) design information and modifications thereto, including closed-down but not decommissioned facilities; (ii) accounting and operating records; (iii) accounting and special reports; and (iv) operational programs	INFCIRC/153 paras. 42-50, 51-58, 59-65, 67-69, 64(b); GOV/2784 para. 34	
		2.c.(i). Description of the nuclear fuel cycle and other nuclear activities involving nuclear material	INFCIRC/153 para. 81(c); GOV/2784 para. 36	

Source: Adapted from "Annex I, A Summary of the Legal Evaluation of Measures Proposed for Strengthened and More Cost-Effective Safeguards," in *Strengthening the Effectiveness and Improving the Efficiency of the Safeguards System—Proposals for Implementation under Complementary Legal Authority: A Report by the Director General* (IAEA document GOV/2863), May 6, 1996.

Category of Measure		Measure	Measures to be implemented under existing legal authority (Part I)	Measures proposed for implementation under complementary legal authority (Part II)
Broader Access to Information	Expanded Declaration	2.c.(ii). Description, status, and location of nuclear fuel cycle-related R&D (hereinafter referred to as nuclear R&D) activities involving nuclear material at nuclear facilities and other locations containing nuclear material (LOFs)	INFCIRC/153 paras. 42-46, 49; GOV/2784 para. 37	
		2.c.(iii). Description, status, and location of nuclear R&D activities owned, funded, or authorized by the state, not involving nuclear material, wherever located, and related to specified parts of the fuel cycle and, additionally, all such activities in the state specifically related to enrichment, reprocessing of nuclear fuel, and treatment of waste containing nuclear material		(para. 51(a)) GOV/2784 para. 37
		2.c.(iv). Information, as may be agreed with the state, on specified operational activities additional to that required under INFCIRC/153 (see 2.b.(iv) above)		(para. 51(b)) GOV/2784 para. 38
		2.c.(v). Description, contents, and use of each building on sites of nuclear facilities or LOFs; upon specific IAEA request and based on every reasonable effort by the state, information on activities at locations identified by the IAEA outside such site	In limited cases, depending on the configuration of the facility or LOF; INFCIRC/153 paras. 42-46, 49; GOV/2784 para. 39	(para. 51(c)) GOV/2784 para. 39

Continued on next page

Appendix 2, continued

Category of Measure		Measure	Measures to be implemented under existing legal authority (Part I)	Measures proposed for implementation under complementary legal authority (Part II)
Broader Access to Information	Expanded Declaration	2.c.(vi). Identity, location, description, status, present annual production, and approximate annual production capacity for the manufacture, assembly, and maintenance of specified items directly related to the operation of nuclear facilities, LOFs, or nuclear R&D activities		(para. 51(d)) GOV/2784 para. 39
		2.c.(vii). Location, operational status, present annual production, and approximate annual production capacity of uranium and thorium mines		(para. 51(e)) GOV/2784 para. 39
		2.c.(viii). Information on other nuclear material and uranium- and thorium-containing materials, including pre-INFCIRC/153 para. 34(c) material, some exempted material, and some material on which safeguards are terminated	Partially covered by INFCIRC/153 para. 81(c); GOV/2784 para. 36	(para. 51(f)) GOV/2784 para. 39
		2.c.(ix). Import and export information on specified equipment and nonnuclear material specified in GOV/2629 and on such other equipment and nonnuclear material as may be specified by the IAEA board of governors		(para. 51(g)) GOV/2784 para. 40
		3.a. Early provision of design information in accordance with GOV/2554/Attach.2/Rev.2	INFCIRC/153 paras. 42, 45, 49; GOV/2784 para. 41	

Category of Measure		Measure	Measures to be implemented under existing legal authority (Part I)	Measures proposed for implementation under complementary legal authority (Part II)
Broader Access to Information	Expanded Declaration	3.b. Planned activities owned, funded, or authorized by the state for the further development of the nuclear fuel cycle		(para. 52(a)) GOV/2784 para. 41
		3.c. Description of planned nuclear R&D activities owned, funded, or authorized by, or otherwise coming to the knowledge of, the state		(para. 52(b)) GOV/2784 para. 41
	Environmental Sampling	For ad hoc inspections at locations where the initial report or inspections carried out in connection with it indicate that nuclear material is present	INFCIRC/153 paras. 6, 74(d), 74(e), 76(a); GOV/2784 paras. 51-54	
		For routine inspections at strategic points	INFCIRC/153 paras. 6, 74(d), 74(e), 76(c); GOV/2784 paras. 51-54	
		For special inspections at the locations where these take place	INFCIRC/153 paras. 6, 74(d), 74(e), 77; GOV/2784 paras. 51-54	
		For design information verification at any location to which the agency has access for design information verification	INFCIRC/153 paras. 6, 47, 48; GOV/2784 para. 55	
		During access under complementary legal authority to places and locations identified below under complementary access		(paras. 53-58) GOV/2784 para. 54

Continued on next page

Appendix 2, continued

Category of Measure		Measure	Measures to be implemented under existing legal authority (Part I)	Measures proposed for implementation under complementary legal authority (Part II)
Broader Access to Information	Improved Analysis of Information	Improvements in the agency's information analysis methods	INFCIRC/153 para. 90; GOV/2784 para. 63	
Increased Physical Access	Complementary Access[2]	Access to any place (beyond strategic points) on a site containing a nuclear facility or LOF, including sites with closed-down facilities and LOFs; access to decommissioned facilities and LOFs	INFCIRC/153 paras. 48, 76(a); GOV/2784 paras. 75-76	(paras. 61(a), 62-65) GOV/2784 paras. 74-75
		Access to other locations identified in the expanded declaration as containing other nuclear material or material containing uranium or thorium (2.c.(vii) and 2.c.(viii))		(paras. 61(b), 66-67)
		Access, upon IAEA request and taking into account any constitutional obligations of the state regarding proprietary rights or searches and seizures, to locations identified in the expanded declaration as containing nuclear R&D (2.c.(iii)) and locations involving specified items directly related to the operation of nuclear facilities, LOFs, or nuclear R&D (2.c.(vi))		(paras. 61(c), 68-69) GOV/2784 para. 77
		Access, upon IAEA request and taking into account any constitutional obligations of the state regarding proprietary rights or searches and seizures, to locations in addition to the above for environmental sampling		(paras. 61(d), 70)

[2] These proposals are not intended to affect the IAEA's right to implement special inspections.

Category of Measure		Measure	Measures to be implemented under existing legal authority (Part I)	Measures proposed for implementation under complementary legal authority (Part II)
Increased Physical Access	Complementary Access	Access, as the state may choose to offer, in addition to that described above, to any location in the state which the IAEA considers may be of safeguards relevance (see paras. 61(e), 71 of this document)		
	No-Notice Access	Unannounced (no-notice) routine inspections at strategic points within the sites of nuclear facilities and LOFs	INFCIRC/153 para. 84; GOV/2784 para. 86	
		No-notice access to any other place on the site of a nuclear facility or LOF when carried out during a DIV visit or inspection of the facility or LOF		(para. 63) GOV/2784 para. 86
Optimal Use of the Present System	Safeguards Technology Advances	Use of unattended equipment	INFCIRC/153 paras. 6, 74(e), 81(e)	
		Remote transmission of inspection data	INFCIRC/153 paras. 6, 74(e), 81(e)	
		Remote monitoring of safeguards equipment	INFCIRC/153 paras. 6, 74(e), 81(e)	
	Increased Cooperation with States and SSACs	The SSAC carries out activities that enable the IAEA to conduct inspection activities	INFCIRC/153 paras. 3, 7, 31, 81(b)	
		The IAEA and the SSAC may carry out selected inspection activities jointly	INFCIRC/153 paras. 3, 31	
		The IAEA and the SSAC may carry out selected support activities jointly	INFCIRC/153 paras. 3, 31	

Continued on next page

Appendix 2, continued

Category of Measure		Measure	Measures to be implemented under existing legal authority (Part I)	Measures proposed for implementation under complementary legal authority (Part II)
Optimal Use of the Present System	Increased Coopera-tion with States and SSACs	Use of simplified procedure for designation of inspectors		(paras. 72-73) GOV/2784 para. 102 GOV/2807 para. 54
		Multiple-entry visa, long-term visa, or visaless entry for inspectors on inspection	Necessary for unannounced routine inspections; INFCIRC/153 paras. 84, 86 GOV/2784 para. 86	
		Use of systems for independent direct communication (including satellite systems) between the field and headquarters	In states where such systems are available; INFCIRC/153 paras. 3, 88	In states where such systems are not available; (paras. 72-73) GOV/2784 para. 102 GOV/2807 para. 54
	Safeguards Parameters	Significant quantities of nuclear material	INFCIRC/153 para. 28	
		Conversion/detection times	INFCIRC/153 para. 28	
		Starting point of safeguards	INFCIRC/153 para. 34(c)	

Appendix 3: Status of Additional Protocol States[1]

State	Board Approval	Date Signed	In Force
Andorra	Dec 7, 2000	Jan 9, 2001	
Armenia	Sept 23, 1997	Sept 29, 1997	
Australia	Sept 23, 1997	Sept 23, 1997	Dec 12, 1997
Austria[2]	June 11, 1998	Sept 22, 1998	*
Azerbaijan	June 7, 2000	July 5, 2000	Nov 29, 2000
Bangladesh	Sept 25, 2000	March 30, 2001	March 30, 2001
Belgium[2]	June 11, 1998	Sept 22, 1998	
Bulgaria	Sept 14, 1998	Sept 24, 1998	Oct 10, 2000
Canada	June 11, 1998	Sept 24, 1998	Sept 8, 2000
China	Nov 25, 1998	Dec 31, 1998	March 28, 2002
Costa Rica	Nov 29, 2001	Dec 12, 2001	
Croatia	Sept 14, 1998	Sept 22, 1998	July 6, 2000
Cuba	Sept 20, 1999	Oct 15, 1999	
Cyprus	Nov 25, 1998	July 29, 1999	
Czech Republic	Sept 20, 1999	Sept 28, 1999	
Denmark[2]	June 11, 1998	Sept 22, 1998	
Ecuador	Sept 20, 1999	Oct 1, 1999	Oct 24, 2001
Estonia	March 21, 2000	April 13, 2000	
Finland[2]	June 11, 1998	Sept 22, 1998	*
France[2]	June 11, 1998	Sept 22, 1998	
Georgia	Sept 23, 1997	Sept 29, 1997	
Germany[2]	June 11, 1998	Sept 22, 1998	*
Ghana	June 11, 1998	June 12, 1998	provisional
Greece[2]	June 11, 1998	Sept 22, 1998	*
Guatemala	Nov 29, 2001	Dec 14, 2001	
Haiti	March 20, 2002		
Holy See	Sept 14, 1998	Sept 24, 1998	Sept 24, 1998
Hungary	Nov 25, 1998	Nov 26, 1998	April 4, 2000
Indonesia	Sept 20, 1999	Sept 29, 1999	Sept 29, 1999
Ireland[2]	June 11, 1998	Sept 22, 1998	

Continued on next page

[1] Updated to May 1, 2002; adapted from "Strengthened Safeguards System: Status of Additional Protocols," www.iaea.org/worldatom/Programmes/Safeguards/sg_protocol.shtml. Copyright 2002 by the IAEA (Vienna, Austria). Permission for republication must be obtained.

[2] All 15 EU states have concluded Additional Protocols with EURATOM and the IAEA.

* The IAEA has received notification from these states that they have fulfilled their own internal requirements for entry into force. The Additional Protocol will enter into force on the date the agency receives written notification from the EU states and EURATOM that their respective requirements for entry into force have been met.

Appendix 3, continued

State	Board Approval	Date Signed	In Force
Italy[2]	June 11, 1998	Sept 22, 1998	
Japan	Nov 25, 1998	Dec 4, 1998	Dec 16, 1999
Jordan	March 18, 1998	July 28, 1998	July 28, 1998
Latvia	Dec 7, 2000	July 12, 2001	July 12, 2001
Lithuania	Dec 8, 1997	March 11, 1998	July 5, 2000
Luxembourg[2]	June 11, 1998	Sept 22, 1998	
Monaco	Nov 25, 1998	Sept 30, 1999	Sept 30, 1999
Mongolia	Sept 11, 2001	Dec 5, 2001	
Namibia	March 21, 2000	March 22, 2000	
Netherlands[2]	June 11, 1998	Sept 22, 1998	*
New Zealand	Sept 14, 1998	Sept 24, 1998	Sept 24, 1998
Nigeria	June 7, 2000	Sept 20, 2001	
Norway	March 24, 1999	Sept 29, 1999	May 16, 2000
Panama	Nov 29, 2001	Dec 11, 2001	Dec 11, 2001
Peru	Dec 10, 1999	March 22, 2000	July 23, 2001
Philippines	Sept 23, 1997	Sept 30, 1997	
Poland	Sept 23, 1997	Sept 30, 1997	May 5, 2000
Portugal[2]	June 11, 1998	Sept 22, 1998	*
Republic of Korea	March 24, 1999	June 21, 1999	
Romania	June 9, 1999	June 11, 1999	July 7, 2000
Russia	March 21, 2000	March 22, 2000	
Slovakia	Sept 14, 1998	Sept 27, 1999	
Slovenia	Nov 25, 1998	Nov 26, 1998	Aug 22, 2000
Spain[2]	June 11, 1998	Sept 22, 1998	*
Sweden[2]	June 11, 1998	Sept 22, 1998	*
Switzerland	June 7, 2000	June 16, 2000	
Turkey	June 7, 2000	July 6, 2000	July 17, 2001
Ukraine	June 7, 2000	Aug 15, 2000	
United Kingdom[2]	June 11, 1998	Sept 22, 1998	*
United States	June 11, 1998	June 12, 1998	
Uruguay	Sept 23, 1997	Sept 29, 1997	
Uzbekistan	Sept 14, 1998	Sept 22, 1998	Dec 21, 1998
Totals	*62*	*61*	*25*
Other Parties	**Board Approval**	**Date Signed**	**In Force**
Euratom	June 11, 1998	Sept 22, 1998